# The Smart Woman's Guide to Resumes and Job Hunting

## Third Edition

By
Julie Adair King and Betsy Sheldon

CAREER PRESS
3 Tice Road
P.O. Box 687
Franklin Lakes, NJ  07417
1-800-CAREER-1
201-848-0310 (NJ and outside U.S.)
FAX: 201-848-1727

**THE SMART WOMAN'S GUIDE TO RESUMES AND JOB HUNTING, 3RD EDITION**

Cover design by Lu Rossman

Printed in the U.S.A. by Book-mart Press

To order this title, please call toll-free 1-800-CAREER-1 (NJ and Canada: 201-848-0310) to order using VISA or MasterCard, or for further information on books from Career Press.

**Library of Congress Cataloging-in-Publication Data**

King, Julie Adair.
     The smart woman's guide to resumes and job hunting / Julie Adair
King and Betsy Sheldon. – 3rd ed.
        p.    cm.
     Includes index.
     ISBN 1-56414-205-1
     1. Resumes (Employment)  2. Women—Employment.   3. Job hunting.
I. Sheldon, Betsy.   II. Title.
HF5383.K482     1995                                              95-24864
650.14'082--dc20

# Acknowledgments

Special thanks to all the smart women—and men—who so graciously shared their job-search experiences and insights with us. Their contributions greatly enhanced the quality of information contained in this book.

We're grateful to these savvy professionals who shared hours of advice and collective decades of experience, especially Janet Hauter, partner of The Summit Group International, an organizational development firm in Indianapolis and Chicago.

Thanks, also, to M. Kathryn Dailey, whose left-brain logic and right-brain creativity lent a balanced and invaluable perspective. And finally, multiple thanks to all those other friends and family members who offered their feedback, encouragement and support.

# Contents

Introduction
**Is This One of Those Sexist Books, or What?**                    7

## Part I
## The Job Market

Chapter 1
**All Things Are Not Yet Equal**                                  15

Chapter 2
**The Employment Game: New Times, New Rules**                     21

Chapter 3
**The First Step Toward Career Satisfaction**                     29

Chapter 4
**Taking Inventory**                                              33

Chapter 5
**Create Your Career File**                                       55

## Part II
## The Resume

Chapter 6
**Your Resume: The Essential Marketing Tool**                     63

Chapter 7
**The Resume Dissected: Elements and Styles**                     69

Chapter 8
**Resume Formats: Which is Best for You?**                        77

Chapter 9
**Case Studies**                                                    **83**

Chapter 10
**Ready, Set, Write Your Rough Draft!**                             **101**

Chapter 11
**Design Strategies: Resume Do's and Don'ts**                      **125**

Chapter 12
**The Finishing Touches: Edit, Edit, Edit!**                       **133**

Chapter 13
**The Final Product: Printing Your Resume**                        **141**

## *Part III*
## *The Job Hunt*

Chapter 14
**Networking and Other Job-Search Strategies**                     **147**

Chapter 15
**Selling by Mail: Cover Letters, Follow-up Calls
and More**                                                         **159**

Chapter 16
**Closing the Sale: Interviewing**                                 **171**

Chapter 17
**Negotiating Your Best Deal**                                     **189**

Chapter 18
**Keep Your Chin Up**                                              **201**

Appendix
**Job-Search Resources**                                           **205**

Index                                                              **211**

# Is This One of Those Sexist Books, or What?

Our mothers never had it this good.

Just a generation ago, most women who wanted to work were limited to a handful of options. A teacher, a nurse, a secretary, a stewardess—those were about the only roles that "nice" women could play.

Today, the sky's the limit. Women serve as airline pilots and astronauts as well as flight attendants. Women are chemical engineers, deep-sea explorers, politicians. We've braved the rugged depths of the locker room as sportscasters, and we've donned camouflage to endure the emotional and physical scars of battle.

Indeed, the gender curtain is slowly, yet surely, parting. Why, then, do we need a special resume and job-hunting book for women? If we're supposed to be equal to men, shouldn't one set of guidelines apply to both sexes?

We asked ourselves the same question. We weren't quite sure that women's needs were all that different from men's. We even wondered if writing a special book for women might not inadvertently reinforce the notion that women and men should be viewed differently when it comes to jobs and careers.

So we asked around. We interviewed career counselors, human resources directors, hiring managers and owners of executive search firms. We discussed the issue with the front lines—the people who earn a living evaluating job-seekers or helping them find employment. Overwhelmingly, these experts agreed: Despite the giant steps toward equalization in the work force, women still face many job-hunting challenges that men do not.

## Special problems, special solutions

What makes a woman's job search tougher than a man's? For starters, sexual discrimination has not been eradicated from the working world. For another, women enter the job hunt tethered by a whole set of cultural bonds. Although times are changing, society continues to raise its daughters to be less aggressive, less business-oriented than men. As a result, we women don't market our experience and abilities as well as we could.

Additionally, there are some difficult job-hunting scenarios that women, much more than men, encounter. If a married couple decides that one parent should stay home with the children, it is generally the woman who relinquishes her career—and must find a way to break back into the work force after years of absence. And although most men work from the time they hit employable age, a good many women never have a need to find a job until late in life. After years as full-time homemakers, they find themselves searching for work because of hard economic times, a divorce, death of a spouse or simply the desire to broaden their interests. With no professional work experience, it's doubly hard for these women to convince employers of their capabilities.

Lest you suspect that a militant feminist diatribe is in the offing, let us assure you otherwise. That's not what this book is all about. In fact, many of the job-hunting tips in this book are as valid for men as they are for women.

But facts are facts. Things are different when you're a woman. With luck, perseverance and hard work, that may change in years to come. But for now, it only makes sense to be aware of the hurdles ahead of you. Once you're aware of those hurdles, you can figure out a way to jump them.

And *that's* what this book is all about. Sexist? No. Just sensible.

## For women *and* men: a better approach

In addition to addressing the special needs of women, this book differs from others in another very important way. We do not simply provide a score of cookie-cutter resumes and advise you to drop in your personal information in the designated spots. Why? Because although that may be an easier way out, it is also a highly ineffective way out.

You offer a one-of-a-kind mix of skills, experience and education. Trying to market your qualifications in a resume designed for someone else makes no more sense than trying to sell insurance with an ad designed to sell beer. A prefab resume may look good on paper, but chances are it won't do a good job of selling you.

For the job search is, after all, a sales game. And if you want to win that game, you must follow the same process that successful marketers use to sell any product. That means taking the time to analyze your "product"—your strengths, your weaknesses, the advantages you offer; getting to know potential employers—your "customers"; learning how they think, what motivates them to "buy"; and using that information to market your product in a way that convinces those customers that *you* are the best answer to their needs.

In this book, you'll learn how to use *proven* marketing strategies to dramatically increase your odds of landing the job you want—at the salary you deserve. We'll take you inside employers' minds. Show you how to set yourself apart from the competition. How to create resumes and cover letters that sell your skills and qualifications like no one-size-fits-all, formula layouts can.

Yes, this marketing-oriented approach to job hunting requires more work on your part than the cookie-cutter method. You must commit to some self-exploration, some careful thought, some time and effort. But after you've gone through this exercise, you'll not only end up with more powerful resumes and cover letters, you'll be more confident and better-armed for interviews and other aspects of the job search as well.

## Who will benefit from reading this book?

In short, the answer is: anyone looking for a job as well as anyone who wants to advance her career. Actually, anyone who wants to advance her *or his* career.

As we said before, male job seekers will benefit from much of the information in this book, although some of it obviously won't apply. But then, all of the information in this book doesn't apply to all women, either, because every woman has her own needs and goals.

Which leads us to a few words about how this book is put together: In each section, there are tips and techniques that apply to all job-seekers, plus information for those who:

- Have little or no professional experience.
- Are recent graduates from college or high school.
- Want to change career directions.
- Have gaps in their employment history.
- Want to move on to the next level in their chosen field.

In all cases, you'll find specific examples in addition to words of advice. We've also included several worksheets that will help you assess your qualifications and pull together all of the data you need to write your resume.

## A look at what you'll learn

This book is more than just a resume guidebook. You'll learn everything you need to know to conduct an effective, efficient job search. And in this third edition, we've responded to questions, concerns and feedback from readers by including more information about interviewing and handling one of the stickiest employment issues women confront today—salary negotiation.

*Chapter 1* takes a closer look at the special employment challenges that women confront and offers some surprising news about changes on the horizon.

*Chapter 2* escorts you inside the employment office for a look at how jobs really get filled—and how to avoid the most common job-hunting traps.

*Chapter 3* helps you analyze your career dreams and set long- and short-term goals, taking the first step toward a more satisfying work life.

*Chapter 4* contains worksheets to help you take inventory of your skills, accomplishments, experience and education, laying a solid foundation for the rest of your job search.

*Chapter 5* introduces you to the Career Card file system, a handy way to keep all of your job-hunt information up-to-date—so you can always be ready to take advantage of new job opportunities.

*Chapters 6, 7 and 8* offer an in-depth look at resume styles, formats and elements. You'll learn what does—and what doesn't—belong in your resume, and find out how to organize your resume for maximum impact.

*Chapter 9* provides case studies showing how women in five different job-search situations solved their resume problems.

*Chapter 10* walks you step-by-step through the process of writing the rough draft of your resume, while *Chapter 11* discusses the do's and don'ts of resume design and layout, covering such issues as type styles, margins and page length. *Chapters 12 and 13* help you polish your rough-draft resume into a memorable marketing gem.

*Chapters 14 and 15* guide you through the next phase of your job search: establishing valuable job contacts, responding to job openings, writing cover letters and getting your resume to the right people.

*Chapter 16* is dedicated to the job interview. It's packed with tips that will help you become a more relaxed, confident interviewee. And *Chapter 17* focuses on one of the most crucial phases of the job hunt—salary negotiation.

*Chapter 18* offers a few final thoughts on your job search, including ideas on how to keep going when things seem tough.

# The end result

To sum up, this book will help you:

- Overcome the obstacles that women face in the job market.
- Understand the employment game, so that you can make the system work for you.
- Create an *effective* resume—as opposed to one that gets tossed in the trash.
- Write cover letters that grab the employer's attention.
- Find new routes to great jobs—through networking and other career strategies.
- Sharpen your interviewing skills.
- Negotiate the salary you deserve.
- Market yourself in a way that gets the results you want.

As a woman, you share many challenges with your working sisters. But you also are a unique individual with dreams and goals that are yours alone.

This book will help you conduct a job search that makes the most of *your* skills, your talents. Whether you're a first-time job-seeker or a seasoned veteran trying to advance your career, this book will help you navigate the often frustrating and always difficult job-market maze.

In other words, it will help you take better advantage of all those wonderful opportunities our mothers never had.

# Part I:

# The Job Market

# Chapter 1

# All Things Are Not Yet Equal

Is sexual discrimination an issue in today's employment office? As much as we'd like to believe otherwise, it's clear that women and men still do not tread the job field on equal footing.

Despite the fact that women now comprise a large portion of America's work force, we still have limited access to upper-level jobs.

"Good Use for Business: Making Full Use of the Nation's Human Capital," published in 1995 by the federal Glass Ceiling Commission, documents the disheartening facts. Though they now make up 46 percent of the work force, women hold only 5 percent of the top management jobs in American corporations.

In some fields, women are not welcome at any level; society clings fiercely to antiquated notions about "women's work" and "men's work." Want a job as a fashion retailer? No problem. Want to earn a living as a construction worker? Be prepared for lots of raised eyebrows and closed doors.

Not only is the career game stacked against us, but we are in sorry condition to compete. Raised according to "female" standards of behavior, we frequently are less assertive, less competitive than we should be. In addition, we often have fewer years of professional experience than men our age because we are the ones who drop out of the work force to raise families or otherwise manage the home front.

Yet the news is not all bad. Those who forecast business trends report that the pendulum is beginning to swing ever-so-slightly in our favor. As more and more women join the work force, we are gaining influence, reshaping corporate thinking and breaking down barriers.

Let's take a closer look at some of the challenges and opportunities that await women in today's workplace.

## Discrimination is not dead

Regardless of laws that dictate otherwise, there is no doubt that sexual bias is alive and well in the work world. Salary surveys have shown for years that women earn less than men, even when both are doing equal work. And when a man and a woman with similar qualifications apply for the same position, the scales usually are weighted in the man's favor.

According to executive recruiters and human-resources experts we interviewed, many employers not only have a hard time accepting women in certain work roles, but actually use different criteria for evaluating female and male candidates.

Employers often scrutinize resumes of female candidates for clues about age, appearance and marital or family status, and base hiring decisions on this information. Men, too, may be judged on age, looks and family status, but our experts agreed that these criteria are far more hazardous to women in the job-search process.

The higher up the corporate ladder you go, the worse it gets. The 1995 Glass Ceiling report confirmed earlier research showing that many employers toss equal-opportunity principals out the window when they fill top positions. Why? Researchers suggest this scenario: Hiring decisions for upper-level jobs are made by top executives—who usually are men. And because people instinctively hire people who are most like them, men favor male candidates over female candidates. It's as simple as that—a vicious circle yet unbroken.

## Unsightly gaps: drop-outs and first timers

Most employers react negatively when a resume reveals a gap in employment history. And because of the roles that women typically play in the family unit, they are much more likely to have such gaps than men.

Stay-at-home mothers may drop out of the professional work force for as many as 20 years while raising children. When the children are grown and these women try to dive back into the job market, the water is unbelievably icy. Even women who stay home only a few years face a very cold swim. Employers suspect that these "drop-outs" are not up-to-date on industry issues or will quit after a few years to have more children.

An even tougher struggle confronts the woman who has never worked outside the home and finds herself in need of a paycheck because of a divorce, death of a spouse or family economic hardship. Not only is her job history nonexistent, she may be unfamiliar with the culture and climate of the business world. She may have little idea how to present herself in a positive, professional way, or even how to go about looking for a job.

And then there are those countless women who pull up job roots when their husbands are transferred to another city. While it's becoming more common for this situation to be reversed, for the husband to follow the wife to her new job, for the most part, it is the woman who follows the man.

This type of gap is usually more easily explained to an employer's satisfaction, but any break in employment can create a less than optimum first impression.

## The nice girl syndrome

Even accomplished, successful professional women often have difficulty expressing themselves in a powerful manner, both in resumes and in job interviews. Why?

Our upbringing is largely to blame. From the time we're born, we're taught to think and act in ways that are distinctly female. We learn to be modest. To be patient. To be noncompetitive. To be nice.

These are laudable character traits, no doubt. But in the employment arena, they thwart us, because they keep us from marketing our talents the way we should, and thus from advancing the way we could. "Women," says Janet Hauter, "continually undersell themselves. It's this maternal programming not to brag."

Many career experts observe a marked difference in the way men and women communicate their skills and abilities during interviews and in resumes. Women typically use soft language and diminish their accomplishments by tacking on such clarifiers as "hopefully," "we thought we might be able to," and the always popular, "it was no big deal, really." We wrap ourselves in shoulder-padded, one-of-the-boys navy suits—but our words betray us.

Additionally, we still believe in the myth that all we need do to get ahead is work hard and be nice. No need to make a fuss. No need to speak up. Surely someone will recognize our contributions and give us that promotion, that raise.

The employees who advance are the ones who crow about their accomplishments, who make their worth known, who demand a higher salary or title. This, of course, goes against the grain of female upbringing. Women are reluctant to toot their own horns. We know how to talk and act as nice girls do. But we don't know how to talk and act as successful female executives do.

## And now for some good news!

You poor girl. Society is against you. You weren't raised to be a winner. The challenges are insurmountable, you think. Why bother?

Because the world is changing—slowly, yes, but changing all the same. And for women willing to go after them, there are great new opportunities on the horizon.

After decades of refusing to name women to leadership positions, American businesses are beginning to realize that they've been missing out—that women, in fact, possess a superior management style. Many researchers, including Patricia Aburdene and John Naisbitt, authors of *Megatrends 2000* and *Megatrends for Women*, report that more corporations are embracing the female leadership philosophy and tossing out the old, male-oriented management style. It's not just a trend, say the experts; it's the wave of the future.

In the new workplace, the traditional male style of management—a brawn-power, boss-is-king approach—is replaced by a gentler, more supportive style. Employees are encouraged to be creative, adapt to change, share knowledge and work effectively with others. Goals are accomplished not in the manner of a military battle, where one person hands down orders for others to follow, but more along the lines of a community picnic, where projects are collaborative efforts tapping into many individual talents.

The new workplace, of course, requires a different set of skills than the old business world. Job-placement professionals report that their corporate clients are looking for people with interpersonal skills, creativity, flexibility and the ability to communicate and motivate effectively. These are women's traditional strong points! Instead of making ourselves over to fit the male, drill-sergeant style of manager that ruled the workplace in years past, we now can simply call on those skills that come naturally to most of us.

## We're at critical mass in the work force

Want more good news? Women now make up nearly half of the work force. We've become so vital to the continuing success of most businesses that employers can no longer afford to ignore issues that are important to working women. Forward-thinking companies are now offering corporate-sponsored childcare, flexible work schedules and other benefits to ease the burden of women—and men, for that matter—who must juggle family responsibilities and full-time jobs.

Another trend to note is the growing number of women who, fed up with corporate rigmarole, have started their own businesses. There now are literally millions of female business-owners in America. These pioneering women will provide much-needed role models for tomorrow's generations. We can also expect that many of these women, as their businesses expand and thrive, will provide leadership and employment opportunities for other women.

## The challenge to you: Play smart and win

The question, of course, is just how soon the rosy-colored scene we've just described will make it from the crystal ball into your daily reality. It will probably be many years, at best, before women enjoy true equality in the business world.

So how does the smart woman deal with the gender barriers and challenges that remain? First, by recognizing that they exist. No, you don't have to like the situation. You shouldn't like it. But the first step to solving a problem is admitting that there is a problem. Once you understand the challenges you face, you can overcome them.

How? Banish your modesty and learn to toot your own horn. Realize that you may be evaluated on different terms than a man, and take steps to compensate. If you don't have any professional work experience, build a resume that explains your volunteer and community activities in professional terms.

In chapters to come, we'll show you specific tips, techniques and strategies that will help you do all of this—and more. You'll learn how to market yourself in a way that allows you to clear any obstacles in your career path, no matter how large or how many they may seem.

# Chapter 2

# The Employment Game: New Times, New Rules

Ask around. Talk to family, friends, co-workers. How many are *not* looking for a new job? Probably very few, unless they're of retiree age. Indeed, sometimes it seems as if everyone is on the job-hunt trail.

It's not just your imagination. For a variety of reasons, there now are more people than ever competing for the same jobs. In part, this can be traced to business trends of recent years. As the economy slumped in the late '80s and early '90s, businesses cut expenses by laying off huge numbers of workers. Rampant corporate mergers and acquisitions put many other workers on the street.

Additionally, people are job-hopping more than in years past. It once was common for employees to spend all their working years at one company. Today, the average worker puts in only a few years before searching for different pastures. It's not purely a case of boredom; changing employers is often the only route to career advancement.

To say that the job market is crowded is an understatement. If you are in a highly technical or relatively new field, such as environmental engineering, the competition may be less intense. But in most cases, the career highway is jammed, backed up for miles with job-seekers just like you.

Before you get discouraged, however, remember that in every competition, there is a winner. In some cases, the people who win the employment playoffs do so because of pure luck, but more often, it's because they have a better understanding of the game.

Over the past 10 to 15 years, that game has been radically altered. The field is different, the playing conditions are different. And because of these changes, most of the tactics that job-seekers relied upon in the past simply do not work any more. Sadly, most people ignore this fact, preferring to stick with old and comfortable job-search routines. As a result, they make their job hunt more difficult and prolonged than it need be.

If you want to join the ranks of the winners, it's crucial that you learn how the employment game is played today. So here are the new rules—and new strategies for winning.

## Rule 1: Don't depend on the classified ads

Perhaps you, like many people, believe that the way to a good job is through the classified ads. Every Sunday, you scour the "Help Wanted" section of the newspaper. When you find a job that sounds promising, you send your resume or apply in person. Whether this worked in years gone by—and that's a subject of debate—there's no question that it is not an effective practice today. The odds against you are just too great.

Employment experts estimate that an advertisement for a single position typically generates 300 to 400 responses. Out of those hundreds of applicants, only a few will get an interview. Furthermore, most jobs are never advertised! According to researchers, only about 15 to 20 percent of the available jobs in America are filled via the classifieds.

Of course, that means that some people do get jobs as a result of answering classified ads, so we're not suggesting that you avoid them completely. But unless you like longshot odds, you shouldn't base your entire job search on this very narrow, employment avenue.

## Rule 2: Mass mailings waste time and money

Many people take a mass mailing approach to job-hunting, sending resumes to hundreds of potential employers. The logic is this: The more resume lines you cast, the better your chances of some employer taking the bait.

The logic is sound. So why does this method have such a low success rate? The problem is in the way that most job-seekers execute it. They write one generic cover letter they can send to all prospective employers. They address the letter to "Personnel Department," begin their plea for employment with "Dear Sir or Madam" or "To whom it may concern," and ask to be considered for "any position for which I am qualified."

Assuming that such a letter makes its way through the personnel department to someone in charge of hiring (which, for reasons you will soon learn, is unlikely), it creates a negative impression. It tells the employer that the applicant: 1) either doesn't know anything about the company or doesn't care enough to write a personalized letter; and

2) doesn't have any clear career goals in mind. Both of these indicate a less-than-motivated, undirected individual.

Mailings can be effective, but only if they are handled properly. Check Chapters 14 and 15 for some tips. The majority of job-seekers, however, take the "form letter" approach just described—and make several other strategical errors as well. In the end, they accomplish nothing more than wasting a lot of paper and postage.

# Rule 3: Look beyond the personnel department

When you apply for a job at a small company—say 20 or fewer employees—you most likely will deal directly with the person who has final hiring responsibility. Larger companies, however, generally have a personnel department—also known as Human Resources, or HR— acting as an intermediary in the employment process.

Final hiring decisions are rarely made by HR alone; this responsibility is usually given to a manager or supervisor in the department where the new employee will work. (For discussion purposes, we'll refer to these managers and supervisors as direct hiring managers.) The task of HR is to do initial applicant screening and refer a small percentage of candidates to the direct hiring managers, who then interview the chosen few.

By handling the administrative aspects of hiring, the HR staff frees direct hiring managers to perform other tasks. However, although HR staffers may serve the company well, the system certainly is not designed to make it easier for *you* to get a job!

## A day in the life of HR

Here's a typical HR scenario. Susan, direct hiring manager of the telemarketing department, notifies the HR department that she needs a new supervisor. She is told to provide a job description and a list of necessary qualifications to Diane, an entry-level HR assistant.

Susan and Diane decide that it won't be necessary to advertise the position; because the company's telemarketing department is known as a good place to work, there already are hundreds of resumes on file from would-be supervisors. Diane will review those resumes and provide Susan with the names of the top 15 candidates.

This is only one of Diane's many assignments, so she can spend an average of just 30 seconds looking at each resume. Not much time for an applicant to make an impression! But the really scary part is that the 15 people Diane delivers to Susan may not, in fact, be the most qualified for the job. Diane, you see, is not very well-equipped to evaluate the applicants.

First of all, she doesn't have any telemarketing experience. So when she reads a candidate's resume, she doesn't fully appreciate the information it contains. She looks at an applicant's job history, but she's not sure what the technical statements and terms mean. And she doesn't know whether that experience relates to the position in question.

So what does Diane do? She refers to a list of buzzwords—industry lingo and terms—that Susan has provided. She scans a resume, and if she doesn't see any of the specified words, she assumes that the candidate is not qualified. Many candidates she rejects are, in fact, perfectly qualified; their mistake was to describe their experience without using Susan's specified buzzwords.

## Any excuse will do

Diane also discards resumes from candidates who appear to be more than qualified. This is on the orders of her superiors, who believe that overqualified employees quickly become dissatisfied employees. Some candidates mention salary requirements that are far below or way above what the company is willing to pay, and Diane rejects these folks as well. No matter that the candidate may have been quite happy to work for the established rate. Diane's focus, remember, is to screen and eliminate the hundreds of resumes in her stack, and any excuse will do.

Sometimes, Diane doesn't even need an excuse, other than her own personal prejudices. It may be that the photo on the resume reminds Diane of her ex-boyfriend's new girlfriend. Or it could be any of countless other reasons that have nothing whatsoever to do with the job at hand.

One way or another, Diane reduces a stack of hundreds of resumes to the requisite 15 by the end of the day. Out of those 15, she expects that Susan will call eight or 10 for an interview. And of course, only one will get the job.

You now can see why the experts recommend that in most cases, you must look beyond the personnel department when you're job-hunting. A far more effective strategy is to find out who is the direct hiring manager and approach that person on your own. (We'll talk more about how to do this in later chapters.) You have a much better chance of making it to the interview stage, assuming, of course, that you are well-qualified for the position.

Mind you, you still may fall victim to personal prejudices or some other out-of-your-control screening quirk. In fact, experts say that once you move out of the HR department, that's more likely to happen. Direct hiring managers are not as well-trained in interviewing skills and may not ask the right questions. They also tend to be much more subjective than HR departments. Perhaps it's easier to be objective when you don't have to work with someone every day!

But you'll have to deal with that subjectivity whether you set up the interview directly or struggle through the HR obstacle course. So why add more people to the chain—especially when the primary job of those people is to eliminate the majority of candidates applying for work?

## A word of caution

Although contacting the direct hiring manager is usually your best inroad to a job, you can't afford to ignore the HR department entirely. In recent years, the HR department has become a much more powerful and more important arm of the corporation, especially in larger companies. Sometimes, the HR department is so influential that a "no" vote from the HR manager or specialist can cost you the job, even if the direct hiring manager thinks you're the cream of the crop. So you must take care not to offend or alienate the HR department in your efforts to make a connection with the direct hiring manager.

When you send a resume or cover letter to a direct hiring manager, be sure to forward a copy of the correspondence to the HR department as well. And if someone from the HR department is involved in the interview process, don't act as if the interview is less important than your meetings with the direct hiring manager. Be as professional, respectful and enthusiastic as you would if you were interviewing with the president of the company.

# Rule 4: Create a network of job contacts

No matter what type of job you are seeking, the old adage, "It's not what you know, it's *who* you know" applies. Far and away, the best way to find a job is through personal and professional contacts. It may not be fair, but most jobs are filled by the "somebody knows somebody who'd be great for the job" system.

The system works like this: Suppose the Brown Company needs a middle-level accounting manager. The word is passed around the accounting department. Sarah, a supervisor in the division, thinks that her friend Tom, an accounting manager who works for a competitor, would be perfect for the job. Sarah sets up a meeting between Tom and the department head. Two weeks later, Tom has the job. The position is never advertised, and no other candidates are considered. The personnel department isn't even part of the picture until it's time for Tom to get his employee name badge.

When you think about it, this system is only natural. An employer feels more confident about a candidate who comes recommended by a respected employee. And the hiring process is made so much easier. The employer doesn't have to go to the expense or trouble of advertising the position and evaluating hundreds of applicants. Many companies encourage this hiring process by rewarding employees who refer qualified applicants.

You can make this system work to your advantage by cultivating as many contacts as possible in your chosen field and at companies that interest you. We'll discuss some practical approaches to doing this in chapters to come. For now, just realize that it is the best—and perhaps only—way for you to tap the so-called "hidden" market of unadvertised job opportunities.

# Rule 5: Become a master at marketing

As part of the research for this book, we asked career experts for their best job-search tips. And when we looked at their answers, we realized that the methods they recommended were the very same ones that successful businesses use to sell their products.

Some job-search counselors object to this parallel. They consider it demeaning for people to treat themselves like products for sale. But you are trying to find a *buyer* for your skills and services, and intelligent marketing strategies can boost your selling power dramatically.

In fact, employing a marketing approach to your job search is absolutely essential in this day and age. It will help you rise above fierce competition. It will help you win the job you want in less time.

We'll be discussing specific marketing techniques throughout the rest of this book. But to give you a core understanding of how marketing can affect your job search, here's a brief introduction to the primary concepts.

## Employers buy solutions

Years of research have been dedicated to the study of what motivates people to buy things. Because of this research, we know that people buy a product or service only when:

They believe they have a need.

They believe the product offers the best way to meet that need.

A woman buys a particular brand of perfume because she believes it makes her more attractive to her husband. She buys a certain make of car because it answers her need to display social status. She chooses one brand of peanut butter over another because it answers her family's budgetary and nutritional needs.

Employers are no different from any other consumers. They decide to "buy"—to offer a salary to a prospective employee—because they believe that person to be the best solution to their needs. Why would they do otherwise? For charity? To give you the break you deserve?

If you learn nothing else from this chapter (and we certainly hope you do!), remember this: Employers, like all consumers, buy solutions to needs. If you want them to buy your product, you must: 1) determine what problems they need to solve; and 2) convince them that you are the best solution to that need. If you fail to do these two things, you will not be hired.

## Target your market

Marketers know that it is a waste of time and money to try to sell to people who don't have a need for their product. They concentrate their sales efforts on a "target market"—a fancy name for the people who are most likely to need and therefore buy their product.

Unless you want to waste your time and money, you must do the same. You must concentrate your efforts on employers who have a need that you can fill. Of course, this requires some up-front research time on your part. You'll need to do some digging to find out which companies belong in your target market. But in the long run, it will shorten your job search and save you lots of frustration.

## Accomplishments make the sale

As humans, we'd like to consider ourselves unselfish creatures. But when it comes to making a purchase—whether it be a can of tuna or a condominium—we have one overriding concern: "What's in it for me?"

While employers often demonstrate altruistic tendencies—they may donate to local charities or provide a nice employee cafeteria, for example—when it comes to hiring, they are driven by the same self-centered motives as every consumer. They are only concerned with what you can do for *them*.

You, then, must convince prospective employers that if they hire you, there indeed will be something in it for them—something big, in fact. And the way to do this is to emphasize your accomplishments.

Consider your resume, for example. It should tell the employer what tasks you were asked to perform at previous jobs. But a job description by itself has little sales impact. It doesn't prove that you were any good at your job! It doesn't prove that you were a benefit to your employer.

If a program you initiated saved your employer money, say so on your resume—and specify how much your effort returned to the company coffers. If you sold more widgets than anybody else in your department, state exactly how much additional revenue you generated. Explain in no uncertain terms how you increased profits, cut costs, improved efficiency or made other valuable contributions.

You must use this same approach throughout your entire "marketing campaign." Your resume, cover letters and interview responses should all focus on your accomplishments. This is the only way to ensure that prospective employers understand exactly what you did for others—and what you can do for them.

## And there's more to come!

If all of this seems a little fuzzy right now, that's okay. We'll explain these and other marketing concepts in more detail as we help you write your resume, draft your cover letters and plan other aspects of your job search.

You should know up front, however, that the marketing-oriented approach you're about to learn requires a lot of thought and effort. But if you follow the steps outlined in the chapters to come, you will increase your selling power on the job market.

This marketing approach to job hunting is not just a gimmick or a fad. The principles of effective marketing have been proven through research studies time and time again. Just as surely as they help corporations market their wares, they will help you find a "buyer" for your skills and experience, no matter how crowded the marketplace, how strong the competition. And because amazingly few job-seekers employ these marketing strategies, they'll be doubly effective for you!

# Chapter 3

# The First Step Toward Career Satisfaction

Maybe you've known from childhood exactly what you wanted to be when you grew up. Ever since you played doctor with the boy next door, you vowed you would go into medicine. From the time you gave your Barbie doll her first haircut, you knew you would be a hair stylist. You saw your first byline on the junior high newspaper, and you resolved to be a journalist or die.

Lucky you. The majority of us, despite the fact that we may have been channeled into a particular career or job direction, often feel vaguely adrift. We wash up on various job shores, but none makes us happy. We know we want a job that challenges us, interests us, satisfies us—but we can't pinpoint what kind of work would do the trick.

If you are struggling with this kind of career confusion, you must give the subject some serious thought before you take one more step on your job hunt. As a matter of fact, even if you've had your professional life plotted out since kindergarten, a mental career review is in order.

Look at where you've been until now. Have your jobs made you happy? Why? Why not? Are you as far along in your career as you want to be? Where do you want to go from here? What do you need to do to get there?

You must establish specific career goals—both for the short and the long term—before you even think about writing your resume, calling your networking contacts or filling out a job application. Setting goals is vital not only to the success of your job search, but also to your mental health and happiness.

In this chapter, we'll help you get started on this phase of your job search. Please, please do not underestimate the importance of this process! It is the best way to better your chances of finding a job you love.

## If you could be anyone in the world...

You'll be spending a lot of time at work. If you don't like your job, if it bores you silly or leaves you frustrated and angry, you'll be miserable.

Before long, you'll be unhappy enough to look for a better situation. And you'll be right back where you started—hunting for a job.

Put an end to this unhappy cycle now. Decide right here and now that you are going to concentrate on finding a job you will truly enjoy.

Think about what kind of tasks you like to do. What subjects interest you, excite you? What activities do you gravitate toward during your leisure time? If you could have any job in the world, what would you choose? Video producer? Brain surgeon? Top accountant for a Fortune 500 company? Or would you work for yourself, perhaps as the owner of a small antique store or consulting firm?

Daydream a little. And don't limit yourself. Just because you've been a pharmaceutical sales rep for 10 years doesn't mean you have to be one for the rest of your life—or even continue in the industry. So what if your family always wanted you to be a teacher? So what if you spent eight years in college getting a specialized degree? So what if you've been home with the kids for 20 years?

You have the right—no, the *obligation*—to do what makes you happy. And this is the time to begin. So remove any chains that bind your imagination.

After you hit on a general career dream, define it in a bit more detail. Would you prefer a casual work atmosphere or a blue-suit-and-briefcase environment? Do you want to work independently, or would you get more satisfaction as part of a team? Would you rather work for a large international conglomerate or for a small, family-owned business?

If you have trouble deciding what path to pursue, there are many books that offer guidance on the subject. *What Color is Your Parachute?* (by Richard Nelson Bolles) and *Do What You Love, The Money Will Follow* (by Marsha Sinetar) are two. You might also consider taking an aptitude and interest test, offered through many technical schools and colleges. Or consult a professional career counselor.

If you can't come up with any answers right away, don't panic. Finish reading this chapter, then move on to Chapter 4. In that chapter, you'll find worksheets that will help you take inventory of your skills, accomplishments and work history. Complete the worksheets, then review the information you've collected. What did you love—and hate—about your various jobs? In what areas do you shine? You should find many clues to point you in a good career direction.

You don't have to get too specific just yet. Don't get so neurotic about planning your life that your five-year vision includes details on the size of your office (big!) and the number of plants on the windowsill. In fact, you may come up with two, three or even more general career paths you'd like to explore.

Just be sure not to be too general—"a career in business" isn't a clear objective. Video production and fish processing are both businesses, but they offer you very different experiences. Decide on a specific industry or profession and determine what position you ultimately want to hold in that field.

## If money makes your world go 'round...

Let's face it: Money does count. How much so varies from person to person. If you are in the enviable position of being independently wealthy, perhaps you do not care a hoot about what kind of salary you earn. But if you're like the rest of us, the honest truth is that financial compensation is an issue of some concern. And although money shouldn't be the foremost factor in determining your goals, it's only logical to find out what kind of salary you can expect to earn before you make a final decision about your career path.

There are several sources for uncovering this information. Most public libraries have labor reports and other reference materials that document average wages for different occupations. Pay scales are different depending upon the area in which you live; it's important to know what people are making in your city and state. The answer may cause you to rethink your career goals, or you may decide that money is not important enough to keep you from working in a certain field.

Of course, it's also entirely possible that you'll find out that your dream job offers the best of both worlds: career satisfaction and financial reward.

## Why not?

Once you have one or more dream occupations in mind, ask yourself: Why not? Why can't you do it? What's holding you back?

Okay, so maybe you don't have the education, experience or training to be a video producer or a brain surgeon or whatever else you want to be—yet. But you can work toward that goal! You can find out what type of experience you need and seek out jobs that give you that experience. Or you can work in some part of the industry—as a gopher at a video-production company or an administrative assistant in a hospital, for example—while you get the education you need.

It may take you years to reach your ultimate goal. But if you are working toward a goal, you'll enjoy those years so much more than if you were toiling away at some job unrelated to your dreams. You'll have the satisfaction of knowing that you are doing something that puts you closer to your ideal job. And even at the lowest level of employment, there are bound to be aspects of your job that excite you, because you will be working in a field you love.

---

We realize that if you're desperate for a job, you may think that this is frivolous advice. You may be thinking, "Any job will do." But it won't—not for very long, anyway.

Unless you have some goals—and some dreams—you're going to spend your life skipping from job to job, wondering why none of them makes you happy. Don't condemn yourself to that kind of existence.

## How goals power your job search

Deciding upon your career goals not only leads you toward jobs you will love, but also helps you land those jobs.

Once you know specifically what kind of position you will go after, you can tailor your resume to match that position. You can focus on those experiences and skills that are relevant to that position instead of filling up your resume with qualifications that may be impressive—but totally unnecessary for the job you have in mind.

This type of resume is a far more powerful sales tool because everything in it helps to sell you as the answer to the employer's needs. It also creates the impression of a focused, directed individual.

If your soul-searching led you to more than one possible career, that's great—but you will need to develop a separate resume for each career direction. You can't sell yourself as a marketing specialist, for example, with a resume that focuses on your bookkeeping experience.

## Goal-setting: a lifelong process

It is, as they say, a woman's prerogative to change her mind. And as you progress through your working life, it's very likely that you will change your mind.

Despite the sexist adage, this has nothing to do with being a woman. It has to do with being human. What challenges and interests you today may leave you cold in five years. A job that seemed exciting and glamorous from the outside may be a real yawn in reality. For many reasons, the goals you set today may not, and probably will not, always fit your life. So although determining your goals is very important to your current job search, by no means should you feel locked into pursuing those same goals forever.

In fact, you should evaluate your professional life and establish new short- and long-term goals on a regular basis. This applies whether you are dissatisfied with your job or gloriously content. If you are unhappy, setting new, specific goals is the first step toward finding a more rewarding path. And if you like the path you're on, goal-setting will help you stay—and progress even farther—on that sunny road.

Chapter 4

# Taking Inventory

Every so often (usually on the day you really need to go shopping), retail stores close their doors and take inventory. They count up all the merchandise they have, then plot a strategy for selling those goods.

Before you can develop an effective strategy for selling your "product," you, too, must take inventory. First, you need to make a list of all the experience, skills and background you have to offer employers. Then, you must evaluate your findings. What are your strengths? Your weaknesses? Your special talents and interests? What, exactly, do you have to sell?

This look in the mirror not only will help clarify your career goals, if you're having trouble doing so, but also will help you figure out the best way to go after the goals you set. In addition, it will provide you with the data you need to create a winning resume.

## Getting started

At the end of this chapter, you'll find worksheets designed to assist you in your self-inventory. We suggest that you copy each worksheet and write on the copies. That way, you can use them again. You may need to make several copies of each worksheet, especially if you have a long and/or varied career, educational or volunteer history. Alternatively, you can simply write worksheet information on blank sheets of paper, or create a form on your computer.

You'll also need to gather together any information about your:

- Work or internship experience.
- Education (high school, college and graduate school).
- Special training (seminars, certifications, licensing, etc.). → Life O Communication strategies
- Military experience.
- Volunteer experience.
- Skills.
- Awards and honors.
- Memberships and activities (professional and social).
- Salary history.

Get out your old resumes, job records, school transcripts, written references, certificates of special training—anything that might be relevant. If you've forgotten salary information, consult old tax records.

With this material in hand, find a quiet work place and set aside a few hours of time to complete your worksheets. You must be able to think and reflect without interruption.

Read the worksheet instructions below and on the next few pages first. Then fill out all worksheets, referring back to the instructions if necessary.

As you make your way through the worksheets, don't edit your responses. Write down any applicable information, whether or not you think it will be useful. It's important that you get a clear and total picture of yourself. You may be surprised at what you learn!

# Worksheet 1: Work Experience

On this worksheet, detail every paid job you've held and every professional internship position, paid or unpaid. That's *every* job, whether it was an executive position with a Fortune 500 company or a stint as a summer-camp counselor.

Granted, if you have been working for many years, few employers will care much about your long-ago, part-time jobs. Most employers say they don't really focus on job activity 10 years past or older. But do detail all of those old jobs here. You can never anticipate what type of experience may get you where you want to go—if not today, in the future.

## Listing your accomplishments

As you learned in Chapter 2, simply describing your responsibilities at previous jobs is not enough to make the sale. You must prove your abilities by mentioning specific accomplishments. So pay special attention to this section of the worksheet—it will prove key to your marketing campaign.

Write down any contributions you made as an individual or as part of a group. Also list any employee honors or awards you received.

For accomplishments, always note:

1. The specific action you took.
2. The specific benefits your actions brought your employer.

If you're tempted to write, "Improved accounting system," give this a little more thought. Whenever possible, state benefits in precise numerical terms—dollars saved, time reduced, sales increased, etc. It's okay to approximate numbers (but never inflate or invent figures).

When listing an award or honor, include:

1. The name and date of the honor.
2. The reason you were recognized—the accomplishment and benefits that led to your award.

If the award happens to be one that few people receive, note that as well. For example, "One of only five awarded during the year" or "First time award was presented to junior staff member."

Some examples of accomplishments are:

- Cut company's postage costs by 5% by implementing new bulk-mailing procedures.
- Designed display that increased jewelry sales by 10%.
- Improved product manufacturability by redesigning outer case; resulted in $1.5 million reduction in annual production costs.
- Won Employee of the Year Award for receiving the greatest number of favorable comment cards from restaurant customers in a one-year period.

## So you have no accomplishments?

Baloney. No matter what your position, if you were on the job very long, you did accomplish certain goals. No employer keeps an employee who doesn't add to the company's success in some fashion.

If you need some help coming up with your accomplishments, refer to old evaluations from your boss. Consider any promotions you received and think about why you were given the job. What were some of the really big projects your department tackled? What was your role in those projects? And what about the small things you did—how did the company profit as a result of your day-to-day work? How did you contribute to the company's success?

# Worksheet 2: Volunteer Experience

This is potentially the biggest untapped area of marketing material to add to your resume. If you have been out of the work force for many years, it may prove to be the most important information on your resume.

Were you a scout leader or cookie chairman? An active PTA member? A school library assistant? A teacher for your church or synagogue? Did you serve as president or secretary of a social club, chair a membership drive or organize your town's annual holiday celebration? This all translates into valuable experience—even if you didn't get paid for it.

Your participation in high school or college organizations (such as Latin Club, Future Farmers of America, etc.) and in professional or trade associations—those organizations related to your job or career—offer additional sources of volunteer experience and accomplishments. Of course, many people belong to such organizations in name only; a smaller percentage take an active role. Employers know this, and so are especially impressed by those who are "doers."

Whatever your volunteer experience, note it on the worksheet the same way you would paid work experience. Describe your responsibilities and accomplishments in professional, business-oriented terms. Focus on how your management, budgeting, organizational and creative skills came into play.

If you've been a long-standing member of an organization and have held a variety of positions from committee chairman to treasurer to president, detail each position in the same way that you would identify different job titles you held at one company.

Again, when listing accomplishments, be specific. As much as possible, detail benefits in terms of dollars earned or saved. A few examples of volunteer accomplishments are:

- With other communications committee members, wrote and published Advertising Club's monthly, six-page newsletter and secured donations to cover all printing costs.
- Each month, provided baked goods that generated $50 in fund-raising profits.
- Negotiated discounts with local vendors to save 15% on cost of scenery materials for junior-high theater production.
- Recruited 50 volunteers to participate in semiannual fund raiser that raised $5,000 for alumni association.

If you're one of those women who leaps to leadership roles and have steered many different organizations or community activities, you should have no trouble coming up with specific job titles and accomplishments. But what if you never held an office or chaired a committee—what if you simply were a "member at large?" You still participated—contributed—in some important ways.

Think about how your actions, either as an individual or as part of a group, benefited your community or organization. Did you make craft items for a fund-raising sale? Did you sing in a community chorale that presented annual charity concerts? Did you plan and chaperone a high school band trip? Don't overlook or minimize the importance of your activities.

# Worksheet 3: Education

The more work experience you gather, the less important the details of your education become. But until you have five years or more of on-the-job experience, your education history is an important element of your resume. If you are a recent graduate without much experience in your chosen field, your educational history will, in fact, comprise the bulk of your resume.

Many new graduates try to fill up their resumes with long lists of courses they took in school. But just as a listing of job responsibilities has little impact, a mere listing of courses is fairly unimpressive. You can (and must) add power to it by adding accomplishments.

What kind of accomplishments might be related to school? Maintaining good grades while holding down a part- or full-time job is one that most employers find especially impressive. Other accomplishments might include being named a tutor or teaching assistant (which demonstrates a proficiency in a certain subject); completing a four-year degree program in three years (indicates special motivation); or maintaining a high grade-point average while participating in extracurricular activities (indicates ability to manage time well). Scholarship awards, election to such academic organizations as National Honor Society and other types of scholastic recognition are also noteworthy.

This is not the place, however, to detail your participation in extracurricular activities. Put this information under "Volunteer Experience" in Worksheet 2. Save any special training—military training, real-estate licensing, etc.—for the next sections.

# Worksheets 4, 5 and 6: Other Training, Military Service and Special Skills

Describe any other training, military experience and additional skills you may have on these three worksheets.

On Worksheet 4, Other Training, list any training or education you have not previously detailed. This might include real estate, cosmetology or beautician training, certification and licensing for medical and dental support services, and so on. If you've had on-the-job skills training, such as in management or computer technology, include that information here.

If you served in the military, detail your experience on Worksheet 5, Military Service. Write down the requested data about each tour of duty.

Do you speak a foreign language fluently? Do you know sign language? What are your favorite pastimes that require special skill? Rock climbing? Jewelry making? Underwater photography? Track on Worksheet 6, Special Skills.

## Worksheet 7: Skills Summary

Summarize your various skills on Worksheet 7. Write down how many years of experience you have in a particular category—accounting or sales or childcare, for example—along with any accomplishments and special training related to that skill. To do this, read back through your completed worksheets and transfer applicable information to Worksheet 7.

Create categories to fit your situation. We've listed a few to get you started:

- Accounting
- Public relations
- Fund raising
- Communications

- Computer skills
- Management
- Customer service
- Sales & marketing

# 1. Work Experience

Make one copy of this worksheet for each paid job or professional internship position you have held.

1. Name of company_____

2. Address and phone number_____

_____

3. Your job title (use the actual title that would be on employee records.)_____

_____

4. Start and end dates (month and year)_____

_____

5. Salary (beginning and end)_____

6. Supervisor's name and title_____

7. General job description (one or two sentence summary of your job)__

_____

_____

_____

8. Responsibilities

　Management/supervisory duties (include size of staff and specific duties—hiring, training, etc.)_____

_____

_____

_____

_____

　Budgetary/financial duties (include any duties related to money—writing a budget, totaling daily receipts, analyzing cost/profit ratios, etc.)_____

_____

_____

_____

_____

　Sales/marketing duties (include specifics about product sold, type of customer base, advertising responsibilities, long-term marketing planning, etc.)_____

_____

_____

_____

_____

_____

Customer service (include number of customers you served on a regular basis, plus their status—retail customer, executive-level clients, etc.)_____

_____

_____

_____

_____

Production duties (include amount of goods/services produced on a daily, monthly or annual basis)_____

_____

_____

_____

_____

Technical duties (any duties that required you to use computers or other technical equipment)_____

_____

_____

_____

_____

_____

9. Accomplishments (including honors and awards)_____

_____

_____

_____

_____

_____

_____

10. Special skills learned (computer skills, telephone sales, desktop publishing, etc.)_____

_____

_____

_____

_____

_____

_____

# 1. Work Experience

Make one copy of this worksheet for each paid job or professional internship position you have held.

1. Name of company_____

2. Address and phone number_____

_____

3. Your job title (use the actual title that would be on employee records.)_____

_____

4. Start and end dates (month and year)_____

_____

5. Salary (beginning and end)_____

6. Supervisor's name and title_____

7. General job description (one or two sentence summary of your job)__

_____

_____

_____

8. Responsibilities

Management/supervisory duties (include size of staff and specific duties—hiring, training, etc.)_____

_____

_____

_____

_____

Budgetary/financial duties (include any duties related to money—writing a budget, totaling daily receipts, analyzing cost/profit ratios, etc.)_____

_____

_____

_____

_____

Sales/marketing duties (include specifics about product sold, type of customer base, advertising responsibilities, long-term marketing planning, etc.)_____

_____

_____

_____

_____

_____

Customer service (include number of customers you served on a regular basis, plus their status—retail customer, executive-level clients, etc.)_____

_____

_____

_____

_____

Production duties (include amount of goods/services produced on a daily, monthly or annual basis)_____

_____

_____

_____

_____

Technical duties (any duties that required you to use computers or other technical equipment)_____

_____

_____

_____

_____

_____

_____

9. Accomplishments (including honors and awards)_____

_____

_____

_____

_____

_____

10. Special skills learned (computer skills, telephone sales, desktop publishing, etc.)_____

_____

_____

_____

_____

_____

_____

# 1. Work Experience

Make one copy of this worksheet for each paid job or professional internship position you have held.

1. Name of company_____

2. Address and phone number_____

_____

_____

3. Your job title (use the actual title that would be on employee records.)_____

_____

4. Start and end dates (month and year)_____

_____

5. Salary (beginning and end)_____

6. Supervisor's name and title_____

7. General job description (one or two sentence summary of your job)__

_____

_____

_____

8. Responsibilities

Management/supervisory duties (include size of staff and specific duties—hiring, training, etc.)_____

_____

_____

_____

_____

Budgetary/financial duties (include any duties related to money—writing a budget, totaling daily receipts, analyzing cost/profit ratios, etc.)_____

_____

_____

_____

_____

Sales/marketing duties (include specifics about product sold, type of customer base, advertising responsibilities, long-term marketing planning, etc.)_____

_____

_____

_____

_____

_____

Customer service (include number of customers you served on a regular basis, plus their status—retail customer, executive-level clients, etc.)_____

_____

_____

_____

_____

Production duties (include amount of goods/services produced on a daily, monthly or annual basis)_____

_____

_____

_____

_____

Technical duties (any duties that required you to use computers or other technical equipment)_____

_____

_____

_____

_____

_____

9. Accomplishments (including honors and awards)_____

_____

_____

_____

_____

_____

10. Special skills learned (computer skills, telephone sales, desktop publishing, etc.)_____

_____

_____

_____

_____

_____

_____

# 2. Volunteer Experience

Make one copy of this worksheet for each volunteer activity.

1. Name of organization_____
2. Address and phone number_____

_____

3. Position/title (if no position held, simply indicate "member")_____

_____

4. Start and end dates of this position_____
5. Start and end dates of your membership (month and year)_____
6. Hours devoted per week_____

_____

7. Name(s) of organization president(s) or your ranking superior___

_____

8. General description (one or two sentence summary of your job)__

_____

_____

_____

9. Responsibilities

   Management/supervisory duties (include size of staff and specific
   duties—coordinating, training, etc.)_____

   _____

   _____

   _____

   Budgetary/financial duties (include any duties related to money—
   writing a budget, totaling sales receipts, analyzing cost/profit
   ratios, etc.)_____

   _____

   _____

   _____

   Sales/marketing duties (include specifics about product sold, type
   of customer base, advertising responsibilities, long-term marketing
   planning, etc.)_____

   _____

   _____

   _____

   _____

   _____

Customer service (include number of "customers" you contacted on a regular basis, plus their status—high-school students, disabled adults, community leaders, etc.)_____

_____

_____

_____

_____

_____

_____

Production duties (include amount of goods/services produced on a daily, monthly or annual basis)_____

_____

_____

_____

_____

_____

_____

Technical duties (any duties that required you to use computers or other technical equipment)_____

_____

_____

_____

_____

_____

_____

_____

10. Accomplishments (including honors and awards)_____

_____

_____

_____

_____

_____

11. Special skills learned (computer skills, telephone sales, desktop publishing, etc.)_____

_____

_____

_____

_____

_____

_____

# 2. Volunteer Experience

Make one copy of this worksheet for each volunteer activity.

1. Name of organization_____
2. Address and phone number_____
_____
_____

3. Position/title (if no position held, simply indicate "member")_____
_____

4. Start and end dates of this position_____
5. Start and end dates of your membership (month and year)_____
6. Hours devoted per week_____
_____

7. Name(s) of organization president(s) or your ranking superior___
_____

8. General description (one or two sentence summary of your job)__
_____
_____
_____

9. Responsibilities

   Management/supervisory duties (include size of staff and specific duties—coordinating, training, etc.)_____
   _____
   _____
   _____
   _____

   Budgetary/financial duties (include any duties related to money—writing a budget, totaling sales receipts, analyzing cost/profit ratios, etc.)_____
   _____
   _____
   _____
   _____

   Sales/marketing duties (include specifics about product sold, type of customer base, advertising responsibilities, long-term marketing planning, etc.)_____
   _____
   _____
   _____
   _____
   _____

Customer service (include number of "customers" you contacted on a regular basis, plus their status—high-school students, disabled adults, community leaders, etc.)_____

_____

_____

_____

_____

_____

Production duties (include amount of goods/services produced on a daily, monthly or annual basis)_____

_____

_____

_____

_____

_____

Technical duties (any duties that required you to use computers or other technical equipment)_____

_____

_____

_____

_____

_____

_____

_____

10. Accomplishments (including honors and awards)_____

_____

_____

_____

_____

_____

11. Special skills learned (computer skills, telephone sales, desktop publishing, etc.)_____

_____

_____

_____

_____

_____

# 3. Education

## High school education

(If you have many years of experience under your belt, you need only complete questions 1-6 for high school education.)

1. School name_____
2. Address (city and state)_____
_____
3. Years attended_____
4. Year graduated_____
5. GPA/class rank_____
6. Honors (valedictorian, top 10%, scholarship recipient, etc.)_____
_____
7. Accomplishments_____
_____
8. Major courses_____
_____
9. Special skills learned_____
_____
_____

## Post-secondary education

(List college, trade school and postgraduate work.)

1. School name_____
2. Address (city and state)_____
_____
3. Years attended_____
4. Year graduated and degree earned_____
5. GPA/class rank_____
6. Honors (valedictorian, scholarship recipient, etc.)_____
_____
7. Accomplishments_____
_____
8. Major courses_____
_____
_____
9. Special skills learned_____
_____
_____

# Post-secondary education

1. School name_____
2. Address (city and state)_____
_____
3. Years attended_____
4. Year graduated and degree earned_____
5. GPA/class rank_____
6. Honors (valedictorian, scholarship recipient, etc.)_____
_____
_____
7. Accomplishments_____
_____
_____
8. Major courses_____
_____
_____
9. Special skills learned_____
_____
_____

# Post-secondary education

1. School name_____
2. Address (city and state)_____
_____
3. Years attended_____
4. Year graduated and degree earned_____
5. GPA/class rank_____
6. Honors (valedictorian, scholarship recipient, etc.)_____
_____
7. Accomplishments_____
_____
8. Major courses_____
_____
9. Special skills learned_____
_____

# 4. Other Training

List any additional vocational courses, on-job training, licenses or certification.

1. Training received/license or certification earned_____

_____

2. Name of training institution_____
3. Address and phone number_____

_____

4. Start and end dates of training_____
5. Name and title of instructor_____
6. Skills learned_____

_____

7. Accomplishments_____

_____

_____


1. Training received/license or certification earned_____

_____

2. Name of training institution_____
3. Address and phone number_____

_____

4. Start and end dates of training_____
5. Name and title of instructor_____
6. Skills learned_____

_____

7. Accomplishments_____

_____


1. Training received/license or certification earned_____

_____

2. Name of training institution_____
3. Address and phone number_____

_____

4. Start and end dates of training_____
5. Name and title of instructor_____
6. Skills learned_____

_____

7. Accomplishments_____

_____

# 5. Military Service

1. Branch_____

2. Rank_____

3. Dates of service_____

4. Duties_____

_____

_____

5. Special skills learned_____

_____

_____

6. Accomplishments (include awards, citations, medals)_____

_____

_____

_____

_____

# 6. Special Skills

1. Name of skill_____

2. Specific training received_____

_____

_____

_____

3. Years of experience_____

4. Level of expertise_____

5. Accomplishments related to this skill_____

_____

_____

_____

1. Name of skill_____

2. Specific training received_____

_____

_____

3. Years of experience_____

4. Level of expertise_____

5. Accomplishments related to this skill_____

_____

_____

# 7. Skills Summary

Skill area_____

Years experience in this area_____

Special training_____

_____

_____

_____

Accomplishments_____

_____

_____

_____

_____

_____

Skill area_____

Years experience in this area_____

Special training_____

_____

_____

Accomplishments_____

_____

_____

_____

_____

_____

Skill area_____

Years experience in this area_____

Special training_____

_____

_____

Accomplishments_____

_____

_____

_____

_____

_____

Skill area_____
Years experience in this area_____
Special training_____
_____
_____
_____
Accomplishments_____
_____
_____
_____
_____
_____

Skill area_____
Years experience in this area_____
Special training_____
_____
_____
_____
Accomplishments_____
_____
_____
_____
_____
_____

Skill area_____
Years experience in this area_____
Special training_____
_____
_____
_____
Accomplishments_____
_____
_____
_____
_____
_____

Skill area_____

Years experience in this area_____

Special training_____

_____

_____

Accomplishments_____

_____

_____

_____

_____

_____

Skill area_____

Years experience in this area_____

Special training_____

_____

_____

Accomplishments_____

_____

_____

_____

_____

_____

Skill area_____

Years experience in this area_____

Special training_____

_____

_____

Accomplishments_____

_____

_____

_____

_____

_____

Skill area_____

Years experience in this area_____

Special training_____

_____

_____

_____

Accomplishments_____

_____

_____

_____

_____

_____

=====================================================

Skill area_____

Years experience in this area_____

Special training_____

_____

_____

Accomplishments_____

_____

_____

_____

_____

_____

=====================================================

Skill area_____

Years experience in this area_____

Special training_____

_____

_____

Accomplishments_____

_____

_____

_____

_____

_____

Chapter 5

# Create Your Career File

You've just compiled a great deal of data about yourself. Later, you'll use this same data to construct your resume, write your cover letters and fashion your interview responses. But what then? What happens to this "inventory report" once you've landed your new job?

If you're like most people, you'll shove it out of sight as fast as you can. And you won't give it another thought until the next time you need to find a job. In fact, there's probably a good chance you'll never see it again—such things have a way of getting lost.

Unless you keep your resume and other job-search materials current, you won't be able to leap on any great job opportunities that pop up unexpectedly. And should you find yourself suddenly unemployed, you'll lose days, maybe weeks, getting re-outfitted for the job hunt.

Now, we're not suggesting that you have to revise your resume every night. You need only update your resume when your professional situation or career goals change, or when you have an important accomplishment to add.

You should keep the raw elements of your resume—the data from which you compile your resume—as well as your list of networking contacts and potential employers up-to-the-minute and close at hand. Here's a simple way to do just that.

## The career file system

You're going to create one master file that will contain everything you need to launch a job search: details of your experience, skills, accomplishments and education, along with names and addresses of networking contacts, potential employers and people who might agree to provide you with a personal or professional reference.

You could just keep the worksheets you've completed as well as a stack of blanks in a file drawer somewhere. But you'll find this information more accessible if you develop a more efficient system: Either use your computer to capture and classify this material, or get a supply of

3 x 5 index cards, a box to keep them in and a set of subject-divider index cards—the ones with the little tabs on the top.

Whether you use your computer or the index cards, you will break up career information into small pieces or "bytes." One byte, for example, could list a valuable job contact, the details of a work experience, or a specific skill.

You can organize and break out the information any way that makes sense to you. You might divide your career information into the following categories:

- Professional Experience.
- References.
- Accomplishments.
- Volunteer Experience.
- Education.
- Skills.
- Other Training.
- Network Contacts.

Or, you might organize according to particular areas of skill:

- Management Skills.
- Financial Skills.
- Communication Skills.
- Computer Skills.
- Technical Skills.
- Organizational Skills.

The idea is to arrange your career data so that if you need a piece of information—say, perhaps, to respond to a telephone inquiry from a potential employer—you can quickly find it.

Each entry should be a self-standing piece of information—don't carry over data from one entry to the next. Once you've compiled all of your career data, sort it according to topic. Then organize it in your card box according to subject matter.

If you use the index cards, a typical card might look like this:

---

**COMPUTER SKILLS**

General Skills: word processing, desktop publishing, spread sheets

Programs Used: Microsoft Word, LOTUS 1-2-3, Pagemaker

Special Training: Completed Pagemaker training course 9/94.

---

Or this:

---

**CONTACT**

Thea Guthrie, Director
Austin School of Dance
123 Airport Blvd.
Austin, TX 78722
(512) 555 - 0103
- Runs dance studio with 6 full-time instructors.
- Called 11/4/94, scheduled info interview for 11/18.
(Referred by E. Barton 10/94)

---

Everything related to your job search will be housed neatly in one place. Here are just some of the advantages this system offers you:

- Updating your job-search information is a quick and simple process. Any time you have a new piece of data to add to your file, you simply jot it down on a card or enter it into your file. If you learn a new skill, you note it as a "Skills" entry. When you achieve a special goal, you detail it in an "Accomplishments" entry. If someone tells you to look them up if you ever want a job, you capture that person's name and address under an "Employers" entry, along with a short description of the conversation you had.

- When you need to find a particular piece of information, you don't have to sort through stacks of papers. Information is easy to find and at your fingertips.

- You keep track of experience and accomplishments you might otherwise forget. Your current resume, for example, might not reflect a volunteer position you held two years ago, because that position wasn't relevant to your previous job search. But suppose you change career directions, and that volunteer work gave you the kind of experience you need to get a job in your new field. Scanning your career file will remind you about forgotten skills and accomplishments—and provide all the details you need to include them on your next resume.

- You can easily sort and organize your career information—a great benefit when it comes time to write your resume. You can take out all of your pertinent index cards and lay them out in the order that information might appear on your resume— or pull up your computer file and view the order onscreen. If the order doesn't seem quite right, you can rearrange until you're satisfied. From there, it's simple to transfer information onto paper in resume form.

## It only works if you use it

Once you have created your initial career file, you must train yourself to update it frequently. This will take some discipline at first. After a while, this system will become second nature to you. And you will quickly realize that the benefits of this system far outweigh any effort on your part.

# Part II:

# The Resume

# Chapter 6

# Your Resume: The Essential Marketing Tool

When major corporations launch new products, they spend thousands, even millions of dollars on advertising. Sometimes, the investment pays off. And sometimes, it doesn't.

An effective ad can make a top seller out of the lousiest product. But a poorly designed ad does nothing but suck up money. At best, it fails to pique the public's interest in the product. At worst, it lowers sales by creating a negative impression of the product.

In essence, you face a similar situation. You are about to launch your "product" onto the job market. You need to let your potential customers—your prospective employers—know that you are available. You need to arouse their interest and persuade them that they can't live without your skills, talents and experience.

You, of course, will not be investing millions of dollars in your advertising campaign. You won't be running a 30-second TV spot or hawking your wares in the pages of a magazine. Instead, you will rely on the job-hunter's basic advertising tool: *the resume*.

Just as sales of a new car or brand of detergent are greatly affected by advertising, the success of your job search is greatly affected by your resume. A poor resume reflects badly on you, assuming it attracts any notice at all. But properly planned, written and designed, your resume can work wonders for your job search—in more ways than you might expect.

## What is a resume?

The term "resume" comes from the French word *résumé*, which means "to summarize." And that's just what a resume is: a summary of your qualifications. This summary should include your professional and volunteer experience, education, accomplishments and special skills.

What role does your resume play in your job search? We put that question to career counselors and employers. Here are a few of their answers:

- *"Your resume is a snapshot of you."*
- *"A resume is supposed to intrigue."*

- *"Your resume is your professional calling card."*
- *"It's the core of your presentation; the first piece of yourself that stays behind."*
- *"A resume should say, 'This is who I am. This is what I want to do.'"*
- *"It opens the door."*
- *"The resume is a marketing tool that allows you to promote yourself."*

Hmmm...a snapshot, a calling card, a door-opener. A tool...like a crowbar? It sounds as if the resume has many functions. And indeed it does.

# But will it get you a job?

The answer is no. No matter how wonderful your resume, how stellar the accomplishments it contains, it will not land you a job on its own.

A resume is just one of many weapons you need in your job-search arsenal. You must also develop a strong network of contacts, hone your interviewing skills and polish your image and appearance.

But make no mistake: Even though it is not the sole determinant of your job-hunt success, your resume is a critical element. A resume is the mark of a professional; employers expect people who are serious about their work to have one.

More importantly, your resume often provides employers with their first impression of you. And it may be the last piece of evidence they review before making a final hiring decision. So don't go job hunting without one. A good one.

# One tool with many uses

Of course, the most obvious and most common use for a resume is in application for employment. But there are several others—some having nothing at all to do with your career! Let's take a look at the various ways you can put this multipurpose tool to work.

### On the job hunt

There are many different avenues by which you can get your resume into the hands of prospective employers. The resume plays slightly different roles depending upon which avenue you choose.

**1. The direct route.** When you send off your resume "cold" to an employer—that is, with no previous introduction—its most important job is to grab the employer's attention. As you've already learned, this is no small feat, considering the stacks of resumes employers receive each day. Your resume must generate enough interest to be picked out of the pack and marked "for further consideration." Only then can it perform its other mission, which is to sell you as the answer to the hiring manager's needs.

Suppose, on the other hand, that you make initial contact with an employer by phone or in person before you submit a resume. On the basis of that contact, the employer asks you to send your resume or agrees to interview you on the spot. In either case, initial interest in your skills has already been established, and your resume's main goal is to help "close the sale."

**2. The employment agency route.** If you are working with a search firm or employment agency, you will be asked to provide a resume. In many cases, such agencies will not forward your resume to potential employers, preferring to draft their own "candidate report," a combination resume and written evaluation of your skills and background. At some point, the employer may ask for a resume—in which case your resume is, again, a "sale closer." But initially, your resume is simply an educational tool. It helps the search firm or agency get a fix on where you've been and what companies might be a match for you.

**3. The networking route.** As we discussed in Chapter 2, networking is an important strategy in the modern job hunt. Your network of contacts may include friends, family, former associates and, often, second- and third-generation contacts—friends of a friend of a friend.

In the hands of your networking contacts, your resume is a matchmaking tool and a sales-reinforcement tool. When your contacts hear of possible job openings, they can refer to your resume to see if you're a good match. If they think you'd be great for the job, they can alert you to contact the employer.

Your contacts may be willing to give you an extra boost by putting in a good word for you with a particular employer. Although their recommendations are worth a great deal, it's even more impressive if they can back up their claims about you with some written "proof."

Say your Uncle Bill does some consulting work for a small publishing company. You're an artist looking for work. Your uncle can tell the publisher that you're a "great kid who draws the neatest birthday cards." But he'll be better armed to promote you if he can present a resume that shows you supported yourself for three years as a freelance artist, working with several major consumer magazines.

## On the job

You can also use your resume to improve your status in your current company, whether you want to transfer to another position, win a promotion or bump up your salary a notch.

Perhaps you were hired to handle one set of tasks but have assumed additional responsibilities. Even a good company or appreciative supervisor may overlook your "above-and-beyond" contributions to the department. It's not that you're not appreciated; it's just that everyone assumes you're happy doing extra work for the same pay and same title. If you don't rock the boat, why should they?

Your resume is an excellent vehicle to document your growth and accomplishments. It offers hard evidence of your expanding role and your increased worth. When your supervisors see your contributions to the department on paper, they are more likely to agree that a promotion or salary increase is in order. And such documentation also makes it easier for them to get upper management to approve your raise, transfer or promotion.

## And off the job

Resumes can come in handy in situations unrelated to job-hunting, too. For example, suppose you're not looking for a job at all; you've decided to chuck the corporate world and start your own business. You approach your favorite bank for a startup loan. Your resume serves as proof of your abilities and responsible nature, which increases your chances of being approved for that loan. In the same way, your resume may be helpful when you apply for an educational scholarship, grant or other type of financial award.

## A mirror and a map

There's one other important role that a resume serves: a self-assessment tool. The process of creating your resume allows you to get further in touch with your professional self.

You began this process in the last chapters, when you completed your self-inventory worksheets and began your career file. This gave you an opportunity to review the big picture, to consider all the parts—your experiences, achievements, skills and goals.

When you write your resume (which you're about to do), you'll turn that big picture into one clear and vivid snapshot. For each resume that you write, you'll establish one specific career goal and you'll sum up all of your accomplishments related to that goal.

This process is not only good for the ego, it's good for the job hunt! When you're clearly focused on your accomplishments and you're set on your career goals, you'll present yourself with much more confidence in job interviews.

## Keep your resume current at all times!

Perhaps your company is rumbling under the imminent eruption of yet another reorganization. Your boss even hinted that it might not be a bad time to brush up the resume. Or maybe after you've spent the last seven years changing diapers and car pooling to school, you and your husband decide that if you plan to keep the house, the family is going to need a second income—now.

Life is full of surprises, and sometimes those surprises—which could include being displaced, laid off, fired or otherwise shoved unceremoniously into the job market—are unwelcome as well as unexpected. During such a traumatic time, who needs to deal with the additional burden of composing a resume?

Likewise, you never know what opportunities will arise suddenly. If you have to rewrite your resume before you can pursue those opportunities, you'll not only lose valuable time—you'll probably let the whole thing drop. How many times have you heard about a great job, then decided not to apply because you didn't have time (or energy) that week to redo your resume? Plenty, if you're like most people.

The minute you get a new job or achieve a significant goal, update your resume. That way, when opportunities or challenges come your way, you'll be one step ahead of the game and have a current resume ready to go.

## Lots of wasted paper

In our former lives as managers and hirers, we've screened stacks of resumes from would-be employees. We've seen resumes with typos. Resumes splotched with correction fluid. There even were handwritten resumes and resumes typed on lined notebook paper. And these people expected us to take them seriously! We did not, of course. A few of these resumes made it into our "Worst resumes we ever saw" file, which we pulled out whenever we needed a chuckle.

We reviewed countless additional resumes as part of our research for this book and found the same flaws we'd seen before. Even those resumes that were cosmetically perfect, devoid of typos and coffee stains, often suffered from subtler, strategical problems that rendered them ineffective. These problems all stemmed from one common downfall: failure to respect the psychology of hiring.

Remember what we said in Chapter 2? That employers only hire people who can solve particular needs? That they are flooded with hundreds of resumes for every available position? Most job-seekers ignore these two facts of life.

## An effective resume must:

**1. Match the employer's needs.** You must determine what needs the employer is trying to solve. Then, you must design your resume to match, to make it clear that you are the "dream employee," the one who can solve the employer's problems.

**2. Stand out in a sea of resumes.** This is not accomplished by the use of gaudy paper, garish type or scratch 'n' sniff devices. Such gimmicks only make you look desperate, foolish. The way to catch an employer's eye is to present a resume that's neat and professional-looking. A resume that lets employers know immediately that you are the strongest candidate for the job. A resume that is memorable.

**3. State your accomplishments and qualifications in specific terms**. This is one of the most important principles of resume-writing. As you learned in Chapter 2, your accomplishments are proof that you handled your previous jobs well. They help prospective employers understand the unique benefits you will bring them. They answer the question at the forefront of every employer's mind: "What's in it for me?"

**4. Be clear and concise.** Employers must be able to find the information they are seeking quickly and easily. Remember, you usually have just 30 seconds or less to get the attention of the person reading your resume.

How do you match your experience to that of a prospective employer? How do you make your resume stand out? How do you state your accomplishments so that an employer understands the advantages you offer? How do you make your resume clear and concise?

You're about to learn just that.

# Chapter 7

# The Resume Dissected: Elements and Styles

Thoughts on composing your resume are probably percolating, and you may be anxious to start writing. But don't plunge in yet. First, let's get an overview of your resume options.

In this chapter, we'll look at all of the various elements you might want to include in your resume. We'll explain the pros and cons of each, so you can begin thinking about whether you want to use them. In the two chapters that follow, we'll discuss different ways to organize your resume and show you some sample resumes to illustrate how various resume tactics can be used to create a more powerful marketing statement. Then, after you've had a chance to consider all of the possible resume styles and treatments, we'll get into the nitty-gritty details of putting your resume on paper.

## There is no one right way

Ask a dozen different experts to tell you what to put in a resume and where to put it...and you'll get at least *two* dozen different answers, probably more. Some folks swear by one type of layout, others abhor it. Some state emphatically that certain elements enhance a resume's effectiveness, while others insist that those very elements are sure to knock a candidate out of the running.

Why is there such dissension? For one thing, because there is dissension among employers. They all seem to have different resume preferences and priorities. For example, some employers like to see educational details appear at the beginning of the resume, while others prefer to read first about job history.

And of course, every job-seeker enters the game with a different set of qualifications, skills and experience, and thus different resume needs. A resume design that makes one candidate shine may make another look a little tarnished. For instance, a straightforward, traditional listing of employment history may work very well for the woman who has been working steadily for many years. But what about the candidate who's been out of the work force for a time? That kind of resume will only play up her lack of recent work experience. So please, if anyone tells you there is only one right resume design, don't believe it.

The right resume is the one that presents your skills and qualifications in the best light—while meeting the employer's needs at the same time. Never forget your goal: to convince employers that you are the answer to their problems. The way you do that will depend upon: 1) the type of employer you approach; 2) the type of job you are seeking; and 3) the qualifications you have to offer.

## Standard elements: Don't write a resume without them

Although there's quite a bit of controversy about some resume issues, not everything is open for debate. There are some elements that should always appear in your resume, no matter what:

**1. Name, address and telephone number.** This information, which always appears at the top of your resume, allows the prospective employer to contact you. Obvious? You'd think so. But believe it or not, we have heard many horror stories about strong job candidates who provided phone numbers that were disconnected or never answered—or worse, forgot to include a phone number at all!

**2. Skills and experience.** This is the meat of the resume, offering prospective employers the most clues about your qualifications. It provides details about your employment history, relevant volunteer experience, skills and accomplishments.

**3. Education and training.** In addition to reviewing your experience and skills, your potential employer will want to know how you've been trained for the role you want to play. Depending on the number of years of experience you have, you might include information about high school, college or post-graduate schooling. Any relevant licenses or certification should be listed as well.

## To include or not to include? Elements in question

Career counselors, HR executives and job-search experts are divided when it comes to the value of the following resume elements. Let's examine each of these "maybe" elements, and discuss situations in which they can be useful.

## 1. A job objective

A job objective is a brief statement that describes the kind of job you want. It appears at the top of the resume, directly after your name, address and phone number.

Many experts consider job objectives a waste of space. They say that most resume-writers use vague, namby-pamby phrases like, "Desire management position with potential for advancement," which tells an employer absolutely nothing—except that this individual doesn't have any concrete career goals.

On the other hand, some say that a job objective is a good thing, *if* it's specific, clear and concise. In other words, if it tells the employer exactly what kind of job you want. Here are two examples:

- *Position as a legal reporter on a metropolitan daily newspaper.*
- *Administrative assistant to corporate president.*

Statements such as these tell the employer that you know where you want to go. They also allow the person screening the resume to tell at a glance what position you're after. And therein lies the potential rub.

Say you're interested in working for a particular firm. You've heard that it's a people-oriented company with great advancement opportunities. You are interested in any entry-level position, but you hear of an opening in the customer service department, so you apply for that, and you write "Customer service representative" as your job objective. Even though *you* know you're interested in other jobs as well, the employer won't. And you probably will not be considered for any positions other than a customer service rep.

From a marketing-psychology standpoint, the biggest drawback of a job objective is that it focuses on what *you* want. Remember, employers are interested in what's in it for *them*. They are not much concerned about your hopes and dreams, cold as that may seem.

When determining whether to include a job objective, you'll need to consider both your personal goals and the type of job you want. You may want to include a job objective if:

- **You are only interested in one specific position.** Your sights are set. You want to be a corporate video producer—not a corporate communications associate, an audio/video coordinator or a public relations manager. That's fine. State your precise objective, and go for it. If only a mid-sized employer in a major city will do for you, say so. But you should realize that you may be closing some doors that might lead to opportunities you hadn't even considered.

- **Your current career goal would be difficult for employers to discern without a job objective.** Perhaps you have several years of experience as a computer programmer. On your last job, you were asked to write technical user's manuals, and this has inspired you to a new career goal: to become a full-time writer for a computer-book publishing company. Because your work history may not reflect your new interest, you'll want to establish it up front. The job objective can provide the same benefit if you have had a varied career, jumping from one field to another to another.

## 2. A summary of qualifications

A career or skills summary, like a job objective, appears at the beginning of the resume, before any information about your experience, skills or education.

While the job objective pinpoints where you want to go, a career or skills summary identifies where you've been. It's a quick snapshot of your qualifications, a two- or three-sentence summary of your resume. Here's an example:

*Nine years editing experience, including three years as editor of a national association magazine. Published author of more than 150 articles. For seven years, all positions have been in a management or leadership capacity.*

Some experts say that a summary is not needed—that an employer should be able to tell all of this from reading your resume. To an extent, we agree. Your resume should make such information clear. But considering that employers spend precious little time screening resumes, it seems a smart marketing move to give them a way to grasp your qualifications with one glance. In a busy office, the summary may be the only element that a resume-screener will read.

Properly written, a summary acts like the headline on a print advertisement—it capsulizes the benefits you'll offer and inspires the employer to read more. And there are a few other advantages to including a summary:

1. It lets you showcase areas of strong expertise that may be especially relevant to the job you're seeking.
2. It allows you to bring into the spotlight qualifications that may be buried in the body of the resume.
3. It gives you a way to stress the fact that you have many years of experience in a particular area—a fact that might not be immediately clear if that experience is the result of several different past jobs.

### 3. Volunteer experience

Your volunteer experience is a "must" element if you haven't had much paid experience. But what if you have plenty of on-the-job experience? Should you include your volunteer activities? By all means. Employers like to see a good citizen, an individual active in her community. The amount of detail you provide will depend on your level of participation. Volunteer experience related to the job you're pursuing will be more impressive and should be covered in more depth than unrelated activities.

### 4. Outside interests

Most employers like to get a feel for what an individual is like on a personal level. Including a short list of outside interests—sewing, jogging, stamp collecting, etc.—shows that you are a well-rounded person with a lot of interests, that you have a life.

Yet this can be a little risky. What if you love to read, but your prospective boss thinks people who bury their noses in books are egg-heads? The fact that you play softball, windsurf and skydive may intimidate the unathletic couch potato who screens your resume.

As with everything you put on your resume, the question to ask is, "Will this be perceived as a possible benefit I can bring to the company?" It's great that you like to crochet. But unless you want a job in a craft store, how is that going to help your employer?

On the other hand, if you want a job in a housewares store, your love of cooking indicates that you will be enthusiastic about your job. Your interest in weight training and swimming enhances your strength as a candidate for a position as a health-club manager. And if your hobby is studying a foreign language or repairing computers...now that could come in handy in just about any workplace.

### 5. Awards and honors

It's generally beneficial to mention any special recognition you have received as a result of your work, volunteer activities or educational prowess. If you have many awards to your credit, you should list just a handful that are most related to your job goal. We know we told you to be proud of your accomplishments—but a list of 20 or so awards and honors is a bit of overkill, not to mention obnoxious.

Awards and honors should only be included on your resume if they are truly meaningful and significant. One expert, in fact, suggested that if it's not a Nobel prize, you should leave it off. (Then again, if you've won the Nobel prize, you probably don't need a resume.) Our opinion is that awards and honors, provided they are not hokey or contrived, show employers that you have been judged by others to be outstanding in some respect.

### 6. Professional/social affiliations

Lots of job-seekers, especially those in white-collar careers, belong to at least a few trade associations. Employers typically foot the bill for these association memberships, so there's little incentive for the employee not to belong.

If the majority of job-seekers have these memberships to their credit, is there any value to putting them on your resume? If you have taken a leadership role in these associations, details of your membership activity are most certainly very valuable. Otherwise, the answer is, "Yes, but."

Most employers expect professionals to belong to one or two career-related trade organizations. You may look uninterested in your career if you don't list your memberships. But at the same time, don't expect this information to carry much weight, unless your resume demonstrates that you were an active member. Employers realize that many people who maintain membership status don't really do anything within the organization.

What about social clubs and organizations? Choose wisely. Involvement in clubs that are known to devote a lot of time to charity and community projects are impressive—you may want to detail your involvement under volunteer experience. However, memberships in purely social organizations probably will not make a strong marketing impact, unless you are working in a field where social contacts are very important to your success. Religious and political affiliations are probably best left off the resume, because of the potential for bias. Yet if you have gained experience related to your job goal through such affiliations, they can strengthen your marketing appeal.

## No-nos, *faux pas* and gaffes

Resumes, like hemlines and hair length, fall victim to trends. Some years back, in the wake of Vietnam, it was considered potentially hazardous to include military experience on a resume. In today's climate, military service may be more of a plus.

This, and other aspects of the resume, will certainly change again with time. That's all the more reason to make sure that your resume is updated regularly! At the moment, the following elements are resume "don'ts."

## 1. Photos

Unless you're an actor, a model, or otherwise make your living from your appearance, your photo does not belong on your resume. Sure, you may consider your looks an advantage. But you may resemble someone the hiring manager dislikes. Also, because of equal-opportunity laws, employers are skittish about resumes with pictures. They don't want to be accused of hiring or eliminating candidates based on looks. Some employers go as far as to cut the picture off before the resume is circulated or filed.

The bottom line is that putting a photo on your resume is now universally viewed as unprofessional. Don't diminish your experience by raising doubts about your professional savvy.

## 2. Personal statistics

It's no longer considered professional—or wise—to include information about physical appearance, health or marital status in your resume.

Nancy Wright-Nelson, general manager of an executive recruitment firm, relates a story about a man who stated on his resume that he was divorced and had two children. He included the date of his divorce, the names and ages of his children, and the names of the prestigious universities the children attended. "The only thing this told me," she says, "is that he needed a job because he's putting two kids through college!"

Details of your personal life are not germane to your qualifications for the job, and it is illegal for prospective employers to base hiring decisions on your marital or family status. Even scrupulous employers who do not intend to discriminate may be subconsciously swayed by this information. So why provide it? Focus on your skills and accomplishments instead.

## 3. Personality profiles

Some job-seekers include a description of their personalities on their resumes. Usually, the personality profile reads something akin to: "Hardworking, likes people, a real team player." Hiring professionals agree that these statements are, by nature, always glowing and biased, and therefore are ignored by employers. After all, who in their right mind would include, "Tends to be temperamental, has problems meeting deadlines, resentful of working overtime"?

## 4. Job references

You can mention that references are available if you wish, but it's not really necessary. Few people can't provide references, so it doesn't distinguish you to say that you can. Should you write the names and phone numbers of your references on your resume, then? No.

However, if people who are respected in your field or known to the employer (such as a networking contact) agree to provide you with references, you may want to attach to your resume a separate sheet with this information. It may give you an edge if employers see right away that some of the best in the business think highly of you. (Be sure to alert those on your list that they may be getting calls from your potential employer so that they won't be caught off guard.) If the names of your references will not be recognizable to the employer, wait to provide them until the employer asks.

### 5. Testimonials

Some job-seekers include endorsements written by former employers, co-workers or friends on their resume. Don't you. Testimonials do not belong on the resume—your accomplishments and experience should prove your worth. Like personality profiles, testimonials are a bit suspect, because a candidate obviously is only going to provide positive reports. Testimonial comments carry more weight when they come in the form of a letter of recommendation, printed on the writer's company letterhead. If you wish, you can attach one or two of these letters to your resume.

### 6. The heading "RESUME"

Employers know your resume is a resume. You don't have to tell them. Use the extra space to highlight one more accomplishment or skill. In other words, make every word on your resume count.

### 7. Salary information

Employers like to imply that you should include salary information in your resume. But it's a fast rule of job-hunting protocol to hold off any salary discussion until you're offered the job. The employer's purpose for getting salary information up front is merely to eliminate you from consideration or to determine how little the company can get away with paying you. (More on how to handle this issue gracefully in later chapters.)

Okay, we've looked at the different components that make up a resume. You should begin mulling over these various elements and think about which ones you want to include in your resume. While you're considering that, let's move on to the next topic on the agenda: how to *organize* all those elements into one show-stopping resume.

# Chapter 8

# Resume Formats: Which is Best for You?

When it comes to resume impact, content is only part of the story. The way you organize your resume is every bit as important as what you put in it.

Over the years, two basic types of resume organization have emerged: the chronological format and the functional format. Let's examine each and talk about which is best for you.

## The chronological format

The traditional and most commonly used resume format is the chronological format—so named because the core component of the resume is a chronological review of your employment history. You detail the various jobs you have held over the years, beginning with your most recent position and working backwards.

For each position, you provide the following information:

- The employer's name and location.
- The dates of your employment.
- Your position.
- Your responsibilities and accomplishments.

Typically, this experience profile makes up about 70 percent of the resume. In most cases, it appears first on the resume, immediately after the job objective or skills summary, if those are used. However, as we've already discussed, this order is not cast in stone; you would put education and training first, for example, if they were the most important qualifications for the job you seek. (More about resume order at the end of this chapter.)

It's important to note that you can also use this format success-fully to chronicle volunteer experience. You can list volunteer positions in the same manner as you would paid jobs, detailing the name of the organization, the years of your involvement, your position (member, committee chair, board member, etc.) and your responsibilities and accomplishments.

As you can see from the sample resume on the next page, the chronological format makes it easy for employers to see where you've been and what you've done. Most employers prefer the chronological format, in part because it's what they know best. They've come to ex-pect this kind of resume; they understand it and can easily follow the flow of information. However, this does not mean that a chronological resume should automatically be your choice.

The chronological format works best when all or most of the fol-lowing conditions apply:

1. You have a stable history of employment (or of relevant volunteer experience).
2. You've worked in the same general field for several years and are pursuing employment in that area.
3. You have advanced steadily throughout your career, in terms of titles and/or level of responsibility.
4. You have had few career changes and have spent a year or more in each of your jobs (as opposed to job-hopping or switching fields every six months).

## An alternative choice: the functional resume

The chronological format allows prospective employers to discern a stable, steady work history at a glance. Which is great, if you have a stable, steady work history. But what if your career path hasn't fol-lowed a storybook trail?

Perhaps you got off on a few rocky roads—your job history is spot-ted with short-term stints. Maybe your original career compass led you to a dead end, and you wound up backtracking. You may have gone back to school to get a degree to start off in a new direction. Maybe you've taken time out from the journey to raise kids. Or maybe you've never held a job outside the home.

A chronological resume will put unflattering emphasis on your erratic or minimal work history—just as surely as a two-piece swimsuit draws unwanted attention to a pudgy waistline. You may be better off with a functional resume.

In a functional resume, your accomplishments, qualifications and experience are grouped together and presented according to areas of

## Sample: Chronological Resume

**Margaret Leary**
2403 Midtown Road
Cincinnati, OH 45207
513-555-0000

**Skills Summary**

More than 11 years editing experience. Extensive professional background in writing, editing, copy-editing and manuscript production. Consumer magazine and textbook publishing expertise.

**Employment History**

1989 - present

**Margaret Leary Editing Services,** Cincinnati, Ohio
**Self-employed freelance editor.** Edit and index professional and technical reference books. Also edit manuscripts for consumer periodicals.
- Within one year of starting business, established client base that includes McCarty Publishing, Suburban Living, Cincinnati Press and Samuels Corporation.
- Achieved profit goals while delivering services at 15% less than clients would pay in-house staff.

1987 - 1989

**McCarty Publishing,** Cincinnati, Ohio
**Editor.** Prepared textbook and reference book manuscripts for publication. Responsible for comprehensive editing, styling, copy marking and proofreading.
- Established workflow procedures that increased the number of titles published per year by 30%.
- Created computer program to allow for automatic style checks; reduced amount of time spent on copy-editing by 25%.

1984 - 1987

**Suburban Living,** Cincinnati, Ohio
**Copy Editor.** Edited all copy for 48-page, bimonthly, regional-interest magazine. Also wrote feature stories, headlines and photo captions.
- Won 1982 Ohio Association of Business Communicators Gold Award for outstanding business-travel reporting.

**Related Experience**

1993 - present

Editorial advisor for "Kidstuff," a local weekly newspaper published by elementary-age children.

1994 - present

Promotions committee chair for local community center.

**Education**

1982

B.A., Journalism, Ohio University, Athens, Ohio

**Professional Affiliations**

Women in Communications
Modern Language Association

skill, rather than detailed in conjunction with specific jobs or volunteer positions. Depending upon your career direction and the qualifications you want to highlight, function groupings might include:

- Management experience.
- Communication experience.
- Technical experience.
- Sales experience.
- Financial experience.
- Customer service experience.
- Leadership experience.
- Computer experience.
- Teaching experience.

In a functional resume, less emphasis is put on when and where you worked. You don't have to attach years to your accomplishments, nor do you have to link experience to specific employers or organizations. Because a functional format de-emphasizes time, it also underplays your age—something to consider if you fear you will be perceived as too old or too young.

There's no doubt that employers prefer chronological resumes over functional resumes. Still, it may be in your best interest to use the functional format if:

1. Your work history is out of sync with new career goals.
2. You do not have a great deal of experience (volunteer or paid) related to the position you seek.
3. You have noticeable gaps in work history.

Take Doreen, for example, whose resume appears on page 82. After sending her youngest child to college, she's decided to return to the work force and is applying for a position as a telephone sales representative. Although she hasn't held a paid job for 12 years, she's accumulated quite a bit of sales experience through her volunteer activities.

If Doreen were to use a chronological format, not only would the gap in her employment history be emphasized, but her sales experience would be less obvious because it would be hidden amid the other details of her paid and volunteer jobs. Grouped together and positioned first on her resume, Doreen's accomplishments and qualifications as a salesperson become much more evident. The skills summary emphasizes sales experience, especially in the area of telephone sales, lending additional power to Doreen's presentation.

The biggest drawback of a functional resume is that employers may suspect you are trying to hide something if your work history isn't sketched out, if dates aren't attached to experiences. Adding a brief chronological summary of your work and volunteer positions helps combat this reaction.

## A hybrid format

It's perfectly okay to incorporate elements of both functional and chronological formats into your resume. For example, if you're applying for a position that requires very specific computer knowledge, you may want to lead off your resume with a functional-style listing of your relevant computer skills, then follow that with a traditional chronological listing of your work history. Just don't get too schizophrenic, or you'll wind up with a crazy patchwork that confuses rather than enlightens.

## Put your best foot forward

Whether you use a functional or chronological format—or combine elements of both into a hybrid format—remember one very important rule: Open with your strongest card. Because most employers spend only 30 seconds reviewing a resume, you must grab their attention immediately. And the way to do that is to present your most important qualifications for the job first.

Ask yourself these two questions:

1. If I were the employer, what would I want from the person I hired? What would be the first thing I'd look for in a resume? A special degree or license? A specific type of experience? Or a broad background in one general area?

2. What would an employer consider to be my strongest qualifications for this position?

The answers will help you determine the most effective way to organize the information in your resume.

## Sample: Functional Resume

### Doreen Holmes
5076 Buene Vista Lane
Dallas, TX  75260
214-555-7890

**Skills Summary**

More than 12 years sales and marketing experience in professional and volunteer positions. Solid telephone sales background; planned and administered successful telephone fundraising campaigns.

**Sales Experience**

- Telephone fundraiser for charity campaign benefiting underprivileged children. Achieved highest individual goal three years in a row.
- Chairman of sales for annual fundraising project benefiting Seneca High School band. Surpassed sales goals this year by $1,000.
- Sales manager of nonprofit boutique selling school supplies and specialty items.
- Sold fine jewelry in an upscale retail shop.

**Leadership Experience**

- Chaired women's division of annual charity fundraising drive; directed phone solicitation efforts of 100 volunteers.
- Supervise staff of 15 adult volunteer salespeople working in nonprofit boutique.
- Elected to Board of Children's Hope Foundation, a 500-member volunteer group serving needy children.

**Organizational Experience**

- Coordinated facilities and solicited volunteers for three-day telephone fundraiser that raised $5 million in donations for local charity.
- Administer day-to-day activities in school-operated boutique; maintain inventory, order merchandise and schedule volunteer sales staff.
- Planned candy sales campaign involving more than 100 students. Campaign exceeded sales goals.

**Professional and Volunteer Work History**

| | |
|---|---|
| 1994-present | Committee chair, Seneca High School PTA |
| 1989-present | Board member, Children's Hope Foundation, Dallas |
| 1984-present | Volunteer sales manager, Crockett School PTA Boutique, Dallas |
| 1981-1983 | Salesperson, Benjamin's Fine Jewelry, Dallas |
| 1974-1976 | Teacher, 1st grade, Gulfport Elementary School, Galveston |
| 1970-1974 | Summer camp counselor, Nature Trails Camps, Lake Travis |

**Education**

| | |
|---|---|
| 1974 | B.S., Elementary Education, University of Texas at Austin |

# Chapter 9

# Case Studies

Still not sure how your resume should look? Which format will flatter your experience? Whether a job objective or a career summary will strengthen your sales appeal? This chapter will help you decide.

On the following pages, you'll find resumes for five women who are each facing a different career challenge. These sample resumes will help you understand the best way to put together your resume in the following situations:

- You're a recent college or high-school graduate with little or no professional job experience.

- You're a homemaker entering the work force for the first time.

- You have lots of volunteer experience, but little paid professional experience.

- You're trying to break back into the job market after taking time out to raise a family.

- You're ready to move up the corporate ladder.

- You're well-established in your career, but you want to pursue a slightly different direction or field.

It's important that you think of these sample resumes as a guide—rather than a mold—for your resume. Don't just copy a particular format and plop your information into the appropriate slots; you need to read the case studies to understand *why* a particular element was included—or eliminated—from the sample resume. Otherwise, you're likely to end up with a resume that doesn't have as much impact as it could.

*Note:* Be sure that you give your resumes larger margins than those you see in the sample resumes. Because of the size of this book, we had to trim the margins to fit the resumes on the page. As explained in Chapter 11, you should have at least a one-inch margin at the top of the page and no less than half-inch margins on the bottom, left and right sides of the page.

# Case Study #1

## "Does it count if I didn't get paid for it?"

Rita kicked her career off to a healthy start before devoting herself full-time to her young children more than 10 years ago. Like many stay-at-home moms, Rita became involved in community activities. Unlike most, she committed herself with the same energy that had brought her such early career success.

Rita didn't just sign up and pay her dues once a year. She became a secretary, a vice president, a board member, a president. She was a leader, directing activities and making decisions involving millions of dollars. She devoted hours each week to meetings, phone calls and planning, tackling all the headaches—minus any financial rewards—so typical of volunteer activity.

Now that all of her kids are in school, Rita is ready to return to professional work. She wants to channel her experience and interests into publicity and promotions and has learned of an opening for a promotions coordinator at a local corporation. Rita knows she has the qualifications to do the job. But after reviewing her resume, she's not so sure her prospective boss will realize this.

Although Rita does indeed have impressive qualifications for the position as promotions coordinator, they're not clearly apparent from her resume. Rita neglected to match her qualifications with the needs of her prospective employer, to market herself by bringing her strongest sales points to the forefront of her resume.

In typical chronological fashion, Rita's "before" resume, on pages 86 and 87, positions her paid work experience first. This immediately draws attention to the fact that she's been out of the work force for years. It also includes an unfocused professional objective that doesn't add anything to her resume. Her work experience—as outlined in this resume, anyway—doesn't clearly relate to her job goal. Her real qualifications for the promotions coordinator position are buried in "Other Experience" at the end of her resume.

Her special skills, although some may apply to her goal, are too qualitative, vague and unsubstantiated.

In her much-improved revised resume, shown on pages 88 and 89, Rita replaced a vague objective with an on-target summary of her qualifications. By mentioning promotions and communications first, she made her job objective clear.

The "after" resume shows her stability, reliability and growth—despite the fact that she has not received a paycheck for 10 years. While many stay-at-home moms opt for a functional resume because of their erratic activity, Rita can maintain a chronological format, which is preferred by most hirers.

---

Rita grouped all her experience together and presented it in reverse chronological order. She bulleted her responsibilities and accomplishments, emphasizing those achievements most closely related to the job.

Rita dropped the special skills section, proving her skills by citing specific accomplishments under her experiences. She did include a list of computer skills, however, as her prospective employer placed heavy emphasis on this.

She also dropped both the "Resume" heading and mention of references.

Most experts advise against highlighting religious or ethnic affiliations as Rita has done. If your activities with such organizations are insignificant to the job, don't mention them. However, Rita's involvement in the Jewish community is significant. In her case, her risk of not appearing qualified if she leaves off this valuable experience is greater.

The final result? A clear and concise portrait of a woman who knows how to initiate, plan, organize, implement and launch successful promotions.

## RITA STERN
2018 Pine Tree Circle
Indianapolis, Indiana  46260
(317) 555-0000

**PROFESSIONAL OBJECTIVE:** A professional position that will enable me to use my communications and promotional skills.

## WORK EXPERIENCE

**Director of Marketing, Kimbrough Credit Union, Indianapolis, Indiana**

1983-1985 — Instituted marketing program, including development and editing of member newsletters, both general and for share draft (checking) accounts; developed service brochures, and performed other marketing duties for $16 million credit union.

**Director of Public Relations, University Credit Union, Indianapolis, Indiana**

1980-1983 — Instituted and directed marketing for this Credit Union, which grew from $15 million to $20 million in assets during the four years I was there. Developed and produced Credit Union newsletter, which was published six times a year, wrote and produced all other credit union literature; developed system of internal communications (reaching five offices and 30 employees), organized and administered Legal Services Program, and instituted and arranged semi-annual employee training seminars, wrote employee manual. Developed marketing and public relations into vital part of Credit Union's operation. Also responsible for marketing the Credit Union to various businesses not yet in the field of membership. Arranged group "sign-ups" and ongoing communication for employees of these businesses when they did affiliate with the Credit Union.

**Administrator, Consortium for Urban Learning, Indianapolis, Indiana**

1976-1980 — Designed and developed courses for adult, post-secondary students; handled coordination of these courses, including registration, space allocation, advertising and communication with students. Wrote project proposals. Also did computer assisted research and evaluation of projects, student demographics and courses.

## EDUCATION

- Florida State University, Tallahassee: 1976 M.S. in Design and Management of Post-secondary Education

- University of Delaware, Newark: 1974 B.S. Elementary Education

## OTHER EXPERIENCE

**Vice President, Membership, regional council of Women's American ORT**

1992-present — Responsible for overseeing the membership operations of three chapters of ORT, an international fundraising organization. Counsel chapter presidents and membership officers, keep updated records of memberships, and aid in promoting the ORT program in order to encourage increased membership.

**President, local chapter, Women's American ORT**

1990-1992      Supervise board of 15 people. Responsible for the operation of chapter, including programs, fundraising, communications, projects. Computerized chapter information using database program. During this two-year term, chapter raised more than $20,000 for ORT and increased membership by more than 25%.

**Chairman, Budget and Allocations Committee, Jewish Federation of Greater Indianapolis**

1989-1991      Committee is responsible for allocation of more than $4 million to the various agencies supported by the Federation.

**Membership Secretary, local chapter Women's American ORT**

1989-1990      Responsible for sending dues statements, receiving dues payments and keeping membership records for more than 150 members.

**Board Member, Jewish Federation of Greater Indianapolis**

1988-present      Provide input, serve on committees and help with fundraising campaigns toward the successful operation of the organization.

**Chairman, Camp Committee of the Jewish Community Center of Indianapolis**

1986-1988      Help in formulation of policies for the day camps.

**SPECIAL SKILLS**

Writing, attention to detail, coordination and organization, some computer experience

**OTHER INTERESTS AND AFFILIATIONS**

Hadassah, National Council of Jewish Women, B'nai B'rith Women, Indianapolis Zoo, Children's Museum and PTA. Active involvement in children's school. Enjoy walking, tennis, bowling and traveling.

**REFERENCES ATTACHED**

## RITA STERN

2018 Pine Tree Circle
Indianapolis, IN 46260
(317) 555-0000

### SUMMARY OF EXPERIENCE

- More than 16 years experience in publicity, communications and promotions
- Direct promotional activity for membership events involving hundreds of attendees
- Planned all aspects of semiannual training seminars for groups of more than 100
- Macintosh and PC computer skills (including word processing, graphics and spreadsheet programs)

### EXPERIENCE

**Women's American Organization for Rehabilitation through Training (ORT),** Indianapolis, IN, 1989–present

**Regional Council Vice President, Membership,** 1992–present. Direct membership operations for three area chapters of international fundraising organization.
- Initiate and plan membership drives and other membership recruiting events
- Promote ORT through community organizations and local media
- Computerized all membership records, which streamlined mailing operations and reduced costs by 20%

**Chapter President,** 1990–1992. Administered local chapter operations, including programs, fundraising and communications. Supervised 15-member executive board.
- Introduced and implemented promotion that increased funds by 40% in one year
- During two-year term, increased chapter membership by 25%
- Computerized chapter information using database program, cutting time spent on mailings by 50%

**Chapter Membership Secretary,** 1989–1990. Coordinated all membership accounting and record activity.
- Tracked dues payments and maintained membership records for more than 150 members
- Initiated program that reduced delinquent dues payments by 10%

**Jewish Federation of Greater Indianapolis,** Indianapolis, IN, 1989–1990

**Budget and Allocations Committee Chair.** Headed committee responsible for allocating more than $4 million to various Federation agencies.
- Scheduled, planned and directed all committee activities
- Presented decisions and recommendations to Board of Directors

*(continued)*

**Jewish Community Center of Indianapolis,** Indianapolis, IN, 1987–1989

> **Camp Committee Chair.** Led committee that developed day-camp policies and promoted summer-camp enrollment.
> - Introduced and organized summer-camp promotion that increased enrollment by 15% in one year
> - Proposed new policies that increased the number of returning campers by 8%

**Midwest Credit Union,** Indianapolis, IN, 1985–1987

> **Director of Marketing.** Instituted comprehensive marketing program for $16 million credit union.
> - Developed, wrote and edited bimonthly member newsletter
> - Supervised all marketing activity and a staff of six

**College Credit Union,** Indianapolis, IN, 1982–1985

> **Director of Public Relations.** Established and directed public relations program for $20 million credit union.
> - Wrote, edited and produced bimonthly newsletter
> - Developed and implemented system of internal communications (reaching five offices and 30 employees)

**Center for Urban Learning,** Indianapolis, IN, 1978–1982

> **Administrator of Adult Education.** Designed courses for post-secondary students.
> - Coordinated registration, space allocation, advertising and student communications for all courses
> - Evaluated and recommended courses to curriculum board

## EDUCATION

> **M.S., Design and Management of Post-Secondary Education,** 1978, Florida State University, Tallahassee
> **B.S. Elementary Education,** 1976, University of Delaware, Newark

## COMPUTER SKILLS

- Familiar with PC and Macintosh systems
- Experienced in word processing programs including WordPerfect, Microsoft Word and Ami Pro
- Knowledge of graphics and analytical tools including Lotus 1-2-3 and Adobe PageMaker

## MEMBERSHIPS

- Indianapolis Public Schools PTA, 1990–present
- Indianapolis Museum of Art Horticulture Society, 1993–present

# Case Study #2

# "I don't work. I'm just a housewife."

After her husband's death, Bev realized that she would not be able to manage financially on the small life insurance policy left to her. For the first time in her life, she would have to find a job.

In raising a family, Bev coached four children through everything from learning to read to surviving adolescent identity crises. She coordinated car pool schedules that would confuse an air-traffic controller. Not only had she juggled a tight family budget, she managed all personal and financial matters for her elderly mother for three years. She coordinated her husband's hectic professional and personal calendars and assisted him with his research by typing papers and preparing spreadsheets on their computer.

In addition to caring for her own family, Bev was a volunteer who was content to serve rather than to lead. She spent two mornings a week at a home for handicapped children, filing and driving patients to appointments. She served meals to infirm seniors. She continues to supervise the preschool care program each Sunday at her church. And for years, she cared for her preschool grandsons while their mother worked.

But when asked about experience and a resume, Bev sadly replied, "I don't have any experience. I'm just a housewife."

After some coaching from her daughters and supportive friends, Bev was able to rid herself of a self-deprecating attitude and acknowledge her value as a potential employee.

She gave her job goals some serious thought. Although she didn't expect to land an executive position, she wanted to find satisfying work in a people-oriented environment. She identified her strengths: solid office skills and extensive experience as a caregiver.

A friend alerted Bev to a job opening at an adult-care residence. The administrator needed someone who could manage the computerized patient database, handle insurance processing, keep the office organized, and exhibit sensitivity for the people living in the home.

Armed with this knowledge and her positive attitude, Bev had the self-confidence to create a professional resume—the first in her life.

Bev clearly targeted her job goal and followed with a summary highlighting relevant experiences. A functional format proves more flattering to Bev's background than a chronological format, which would accentuate her lack of work experience. The functional format allows her to group office and computer skills she's gathered, and features her varied caregiving experiences. After listing her skills, Bev then added a brief chronological rundown of her volunteer history. She also listed an award that should be significant to her prospective employer. It indicates that she's likely to be valuable as a paid employee.

# BEVERLY GOODRICH

1101 River Way
Jacksonville, FL 32203
(904) 555-7890

## Job Objective

Administrative assistant in a residence for handicapped adults

## Skills Summary

- 12 years experience providing office support in a residence for handicapped children
- Excellent office skills, including computer skills, typing (80 wpm), filing and familiarity with medical insurance processing
- Strong experience in caregiving for children and senior citizens

## Office and Organizational Experience

- Maintain patient files for group home with 150 full-time residents
- Complete and process medical and dental insurance claim forms
- Initiated and implemented new filing system to make patient information more accessible to staff of group home
- Coordinated personal and professional schedule for university department head
- Developed, typed and proofread spreadsheets for research papers for university department head

## Computer Experience

- Trained administrators and therapists at group home on Lotus 1-2-3, saving outside training expenses of more than $1,000
- Produced spreadsheets, reports and other documents using Lotus 1-2-3, Ami Pro and Microsoft Word
- Operational knowledge of Macintosh and IBM-PC computers

## Social Services Experience

- Drive handicapped children to medical appointments
- Handled personal care and finances of elderly woman for three years
- Served hot meals to elderly in their homes for nine years
- Supervise preschool children at church daycare
- Provided in-home daycare for two children for five years

## Volunteer History

- Office support, New Hope Children's Center, Jacksonville, 1983–present
- Preschool daycare supervisor, All Saints Church, Jacksonville, 1980–present
- Driver/server, Meals on Wheels, Jacksonville, 1981–1990
- Administrative support, Dr. Stan Goodrich, Jacksonville University, 1982–1990

## Awards and Honors

Volunteer of the Year, New Hope Children's Center, 1992. Awarded for outstanding service to center caring for handicapped children.

# Case Study #3

## Fresh out of school and into the big time

In a few months, Kristen Harris will close the door on college life and move on to the "real world." Graduating with a degree in business administration and management information systems, Kristen hopes to land an entry-level position as a computer programmer/analyst. She's most interested in the area of financial database systems. Her long-term goal is to become an MIS manager for a large international corporation.

Like many college students, Kristen has only classroom experience in her chosen field. Her work experience won't be a big plus, because it's unrelated to her job goal. So Kristen must instead play up her three strongest sales points:

1. Her soon-to-be-awarded degree in Business Administration.
2. Her scholastic accomplishments.
3. Her campus leadership experience (offices held in her sorority).

Kristen will be competing with thousands of other college seniors with similar credentials. Leadership experience, however, is less common, and employers are always looking for people willing to take on those roles. By detailing her leadership skills, Kristen can set herself apart.

In structuring her resume, shown on page 93, Kristen presents her strongest qualifications first. Her skills summary tells employers that she not only has the basic qualifications needed in an entry-level position, but also offers the advantage of being an organizational leader.

The next section delineates Kristen's specific computer skills. This will be vital to employers; they will want to know if she is familiar with their types of systems. Because Kristen plans to focus on the financial systems sector, she mentions her coursework in that area as well.

Third on the resume is Kristen's educational information, placed here because after her computer skills, her degree and her grades are two of her most important qualifications.

Kristen emphasizes her leadership experience by presenting it in the form of work experience, including job titles, duties and accomplishments.

In the next section, Kristen lists honors and awards, mentioning two academic scholarships she has received.

Next-to-last is a quick rundown of professional work experience. Here Kristen includes only employers' names, locations and her job title. This experience offers the least potential benefit to the employer, so it appears at the end.

The last line of the resume tells employers that references can be obtained through the university placement center. This is important because it helps corporations with on-campus recruiting. If Kristen weren't registered in that system, she could skip mention of references.

**KRISTEN B. HARRIS**

Address until May 20, 1996:
409 University Street
Bowling Green, OH 43403
(419) 555-5225

Address after May 20, 1996:
309 Kingston Drive
Bethesda, OH 43719
(614) 555-3202

## Summary of Qualifications

Will receive bachelor's degree in Business Administration/MIS in May 1996. Knowledge of systems analysis and programming for business applications. Experience in organizational leadership, publicity and communications.

## Computer Skills

- Knowledge of BASIC, COBOL and Assembler languages
- Designed and programmed inventory and reporting system as part of classroom project
- Extensive coursework in the following areas:
    - System design and methodology
    - Relational database design and management
    - Business management and operations
    - Finance and accounting systems

## Education

- Business Administration, Management Information Systems; Bowling Green State University, Bowling Green, OH; Graduation date, May 1996; 3.74/4.0 GPA
- Cadiz High School, Cadiz, OH; Graduated May 1992; 3.8/4.0 GPA

## Leadership Experience

Kappa Delta Sorority, Bowling Green State University, Bowling Green, OH

President, 1995-present
- Served as liaison between local chapter and national officers
- Coordinated national leadership school, organizing seminars and workshops for regional chapter officers

Public Relations Chair, 1994-95
- Initiated and implemented all campus and community publicity
- Founded Outstanding Alumna program to increase alumna support

Editor, 1993-94
- Wrote articles and shot photographs for national sorority magazine

## Honors and Awards

- Ohio Valley Panhellenic Council Scholarship Recipient, 1993, awarded for scholastic achievement and university activities
- Howard-Plouck Scholarship Recipient, 1992, awarded for scholastic achievement

## Employment History

- Michael and Mae's Games, Bethesda, OH; Summers 1994 and 1995; factory worker
- Pizza Hut, Bethesda, OH; Summers 1992 and 1993; waitress/hostess
- Bowling Green Alumni Center, Bowling Green, OH; Spring 1992; telemarketing fundraiser

*References available from Bowling Green State University Placement Center*

## Case Study #4

## Moving up the corporate ladder

For the sake of demonstration, let's imagine that instead of being poised for her first step into the working world, Kristen, our new college graduate from the last case study, is five years into her career. Same background, same educational experiences—only this time, Kristen has solid professional history under her belt.

Since graduating from college, Kristen has held three jobs, all in the field of systems programming and analysis. In all three jobs, one of her responsibilities was to train company employees on how to use various computer systems. This experience has caused her to rethink her original long-term goal, which, if you remember, was to be an MIS department manager. She has so enjoyed the teaching aspects of her jobs that she's decided to move into the training field. There's an opening for a systems trainer in her company, and she's going to apply.

How does Kristen's new resume differ from her initial pregraduation resume—aside from the obvious addition of detailing three professional positions? Well, first of all, the sorority-related leadership experience is dropped. She doesn't need it. The new accomplishments and responsibilities Kristen describes in her experience profile should be adequate to convince employers of her leadership capabilities.

Second, her skills summary is revised, not only to show her years of experience, but also to emphasize her training background. Her experience profile is also tailored to the training position; Kristen makes a point to include the fact that she performed some form of training in all of her positions.

Of course, Kristen gained a lot of systems programming and analysis experience throughout her three jobs, too. So why isn't that experience highlighted more? You guessed it—it's not as relevant to her job goal as her training experience.

However, the systems trainer will need to have a broad knowledge of many different types of software and programming languages, so Kristen includes a list of those systems in which she is proficient. It follows her experience profile here, because although it is important, it is less so than her training experience.

Kristen has elected not to include any of the summer jobs listed on her pre-graduation resume. Now that she has solid experience in her field, those jobs are even more irrelevant than before. Also deleted from this new resume are high school education data and scholarship awards. The grade point average in her college-education listing and her accomplishments at work now serve as ample proof of her smarts.

# KRISTEN HARRIS

3234 Seneca Drive
Houston, TX 77082
(713) 555-2310

**SUMMARY**

Five years experience in systems analysis and programming for international transportation and energy corporations. Strong background in user training and support documentation. Experience in major programming languages, operating hardware and software.

**EXPERIENCE**

8/95–present

Global Airlines, Houston
**Senior Systems Analyst,** Sales Administration and Program Development. Develop database programming to meet management and field-sales information needs.
- Design and implement sales systems at company's regional technical centers
- Train sales staff on use of new programs
- Created voice-automation system that increased telemarketing department productivity and allowed 15% staffing reduction

8/90–8/95

World Oil Company, Houston
**Purchasing Systems Analyst,** Corporate Procurement. Promoted from Systems Analyst position in 4/93. Programmed management reporting systems for purchasing department.
- Served as liaison between system users and technical support group
- Trained field system users
- Created invoice-reconciliation program that resulted in capturing an average of 5K per month in vendor overcharges

**Systems Analyst,** Computer Services Organization, 8/90–4/93. Designed and implemented systems for crude-oil acquisition applications.
- Wrote computer procedure specifications and user manuals
- Designed and supervised programming of tracking system that determined more cost-effective transportation routes

**SYSTEMS PROFICIENCY**

Hardware: IBM 3090, MVS Operating System/JES2, IBM PS/2 Model 55

Programming Languages: NATURAL/ADABAS, JCL, SAR, SAS, FOCUS, QMF/SQUL with DB2, UCC7, ROSCOE, TSO, ISPF, Predict, COBOL, BASIC, PL/I, IBM ASSEMBLER

PC Software: DBase III+, LOTUS Release 3, Harvard Graphics, LOTUS Freelance Plus, DOS, PCTools, PC Focus

**EDUCATION**

B.S., Business Administration/MIS, May 1990
Bowling Green State University, Bowling Green, OH, 3.74/4.0 GPA

# Case Study #5
# "I need a change!"

Sandra is at a career crossroad. Having spent all of her professional life in business administration, she's decided to set off on a new career direction. She wants to become director of a nonprofit organization. Sandra's taken a winding route to this turning point. She earned a degree in general business and has held several administrative support positions. A few years ago, she went back to school and earned a teaching degree. But by the time she received her certification, she discovered that the classroom was not the right environment for her.

Reviewing Sandra's "before" resume, shown on page 97, it's hard to imagine that she would be qualified for the position she wants. You'd never know that she has experience in virtually all aspects of administering a volunteer organization! She mentions volunteer experience, but it's brief and buried. The emphasis is on her jobs in office administration and her education—neither of which are most relevant to her new career goal.

## From unfocused hodgepodge...

There are other problems with Sandra's resume, too. The objective lacks focus, there are no accomplishments to provide marketing punch and personal data is included. Sandra has also mixed styles; dates are presented in one fashion in the experience section and in another style under the community activities section.

## ...to a bull's-eye resume

The "after" resume, on pages 98 and 99, eliminates these flaws and shifts emphasis to Sandra's vast volunteer experience. The result is a marketing vehicle that will be more effective at getting Sandra to her new career destination.

Sandra puts experience related to nonprofit organization administration first, both in the skills summary and in the experience profile. Her office administration and educational background appear last because they're less important to her goals.

Volunteer accomplishments are presented in specific, businesslike terms. Notice the headline "Nonprofit/Volunteer Organization Experience." Another headline she could have considered is "Volunteer Experience." The first has a slightly more businesslike edge. The emphasis is on her nonprofit sector experience.

The type style puts more emphasis on her job titles, showing that Sandra has experience in many areas of organizational administration.

The first position in Sandra's volunteer experience profile seems less impressive than others. But it's important because it shows that Sandra jumped into her community's volunteer circle soon after relocating.

## Sandra J. Martinez

1655 Glenn Ave.
Lehigh Acres, FL 33936
(813) 555-9133

**Objective:** A career in volunteer organization management.

**Experience:** **Ingle's Bookstore Cafe, Fort Myers, Florida, Bookseller/Assistant Manager, 1994-present:** Responsible for managing daily operations, assigning duties, selling books, buying sidelines, merchandising and special projects. Also responsible for investigating and resolving all customer complaints.

**Sumpter Sports Manufacturing, Avon Lake, Florida, Executive Assistant, 1990-1992:** Personal assistant to Vice President of International Operation for $40 million sports-equipment manufacturing business. Coordinated manufacturing, shipping, purchasing, accounts receivable and sales activities. Prepared financial reports and projections. Managed all records. Handled international customer communications.

**Holmes Motors, Avon Lake, Florida, Corporate Officer and Administrative Assistant, 1985-1990:** Corporate officer (Secretary) responsible for financial co-signing, meeting minutes and coordination of legal matters. Responsible for resolution of all warranty claims. Implemented computerized accounting system.

**Cameron Container Company, Miami, Florida, Office Administrator, 1984-1985:** Learned and managed bookkeeping and other financial functions. Managed day-to-day office systems. Performed inside sales duties.

**Education & Teaching:** University of Miami, Coral Gables, Florida, B.S. (Office Administration), 1980-1984
- Emphasis in English and general business
- Student teacher in high school literature class

**Community Activities:**
- Membership Committee, Fort Myers Historical Society
- Event Coordinator, Chamber of Commerce, Avon Lake, Florida
- Board of Directors/Executive Committee, Tipton County YWCA, Avon Lake, Florida
- Catering Chairperson, Tipton County YWCA, Avon Lake, Florida
- Fundraising Committee Member, Tipton County YWCA , Avon Lake, Florida
- Publicity Chairperson, Tipton County YWCA, Avon Lake, Florida

**Personal:** Born June 2, 1962; single; excellent health.
Interests include golf, cooking, music, literature, travel.

**References:** Upon request.

## SANDRA J. MARTINEZ

1655 Glenn Ave.
Lehigh Acres, FL 33936
(813) 555-9133

SUMMARY OF EXPERIENCE

Six years experience in event-planning, fundraising, administration and publicity for nonprofit organizations. More than 11 years experience in business administration for retail and manufacturing corporations.

NONPROFIT/VOLUNTEER ORGANIZATION EXPERIENCE

1994-present
*Fort Myers Historical Society, Fort Myers, Florida*
**Membership Committee Member.** Planned and organized programs and events to attract and retain members.
• Coordinated annual new member reception for 125 people.

1989-1995
*Tipton County YWCA, Avon Lake, Florida*
**Board of Directors and Executive Committee,** 1989-1995. Helped establish area's first YWCA. Developed organizational programs, procedures and policies, and monitored trustees responsible for constructing $3 million recreational facility.
• With other board members, led effort that raised $2.5 million in two years from community of 12,000 people.
• Elected to Board and Executive Committee for five years.

**Catering Chairperson,** 1992-1995. Organized banquet-catering facility that accommodates groups of 200 people. Established facility procedures, purchased supplies, created cost-effective menus and supervised volunteer workers.
• Equipped kitchen at 10% under budget ($9,000 total expenditure).

**Fundraising Chairperson,** 1992-1993. Managed efforts to raise funds for facility construction and operation. Established donor list and projected individual donation levels. Contracted and supervised professional fundraiser.
• Raised $10,000 in donations through personal solicitations of community business leaders and private individuals.

**Publicity Chairperson,** 1989-1991. Created and implemented programs to advertise organization and acquire members and funds.
• Wrote and published monthly member newsletter; also secured donations to cover newsletter production costs.
• Conceived and organized marketing campaigns that resulted in 400 new members in a one-year period. Members acquired during this time received no services in exchange for membership fees (YWCA facilities not yet built).

1989-1992
*Avon Lake Chamber of Commerce, Avon Lake, Florida*
**Event Coordinator.** Coordinated annual city-wide Halloween party to provide concerned parents with an alternative to traditional trick-or-treating. Organized volunteers, secured permits and planned all activities, including a parade.
• Organized the first event of this kind in the city.

(continued)

PROFESSIONAL BUSINESS EXPERIENCE

1994-present
*Ingle's Bookstore Cafe, Fort Myers, Florida*
**Assistant Manager/Bookseller.** Manage daily operations of bookstore and cafe. Supervise 30 employees, merchandise goods and buy all non-book sidelines.
• Suggested and implemented store's first sales promotion. Effort tripled weekly sales totals while generating greater income than suppliers' merchandise return programs.
• Promoted from initial hire position (bookseller) to supervisor after one month of employment; promoted to assistant manager four months later.

1990-1992
*Sumpter Sports Manufacturing, Avon Lake, Florida*
**Executive Assistant.** Assistant to vice president of International Operations for $40 million toy-manufacturing business. Prepared financial reports and projections; handled international client communications; coordinated manufacturing, shipping, purchasing, accounts receivable and sales activities.
• Developed company's first system for tracking and enforcing collection of royalties from foreign licensees, resulting in improved collection rates.

1985-1990
*Holmes Motors, Avon Lake, Florida*
**Corporate Officer and Administrative Assistant.** As Corporate Secretary, co-signed financial documents, kept corporate minutes and coordinated resolution of legal matters related to medium-sized car dealership. Also assisted with daily dealership operations, including bookkeeping and customer relations.
• Created computerized accounting and business-operations system that reduced need for outside accounting services.

1984-1985
*Cameron Container Company, Miami, Florida*
**Office Administrator.** Handled all bookkeeping and financial functions for medium-sized packaging manufacturer. Also managed day-to-day office systems and performed inside sales.

EDUCATION AND CERTIFICATION

**Florida Teaching Certification** in Business and English, 1994, Florida University-Fort Myers, Florida
**B.S. in Office Administration,** 1984, University of Miami, Coral Gables, Florida

# Chapter 10

# Ready, Set, Write
# Your Rough Draft!

Finally! It's time to write the rough draft of your resume. Grab your career file and shut the door on all distractions. Then turn on your word processor, plug in your typewriter or get out your paper and pencil.

We've divided this chapter into two parts. Part one walks you through the steps of writing a *chronological* resume; part two shows you the specifics of writing a *functional* resume.

Before we begin, here are three important reminders:

1. **Tailor information to your job goal.** Emphasize those qualifications most relevant to the kind of position you want. If you are pursuing two or more different career goals, you need to write a separate resume for each. Remember that you are selling yourself as the answer to a specific need—and your resume should address that need as closely as possible.

2. **Make every word count!** Keep in mind that prospective employers will spend less than 30 seconds reviewing your resume. You must keep it clear, concise and focused on the information that will sell you best. Give priority to the most meaningful of your qualifications, even if it means excluding others.

3. **This is a rough draft.** Don't worry about getting your words in perfect shape yet. Pay more attention to content than style for now.

Although we'll address the various elements of each type of resume in an order in which they might logically fall, remember that you are by no means locked into that order. As you learned in previous chapters, you should arrange elements in whatever order makes the strongest marketing statement. In other words, make prominent your most important qualifications and experience.

## A few words about length and style

Because we're only concerned with completing a rough draft of your resume, we won't get into the specifics of type styles, page layouts, etc., in this chapter. But you may want to take a brief look at Chapter 11, where these subjects are covered in detail, or refer back to the sample resumes in Chapter 9, so that you can get an idea of how you want your finished resume to look.

There is, however, one style rule to consider at this point: length. Your resume should be a maximum of two pages—two easily readable pages. Not only will most employers not bother to read anything longer, but a resume exceeding two pages will probably be a mark against you. Employers assume that someone who can't sum up her qualifications in two pages or less doesn't have the organizational skills or powers of communication it takes to succeed in today's fast-paced business climate.

## A few words about words

Remember back in Chapter 1, when we talked about how women typically use "soft" language to describe their skills and accomplishments? Take special care to fight this tendency as you write your resume. Use strong, action-oriented words and succinct, tight phrases.

When detailing current positions, use the present tense. When describing previous experiences, use past tense. And forget about what your English teachers said about writing in complete sentences. Resume grammar is different. Use short phrases, and leave out unnecessary articles, such as "I," "the," "an," etc.

For example, instead of:

*I sold more goods than any other employee in the store during one year.*

You should write:

*Achieved store's highest annual sales total.*

## And a note about punctuation

This is another area in which everyone disagrees. For example, some experts instruct you to put a comma between the month and year, as in "May, 1990," while others insist it's not needed, preferring "May 1990."

Thankfully, this is also not a very critical issue. We can't imagine employers caring a bit about which comma rule you adopt. The only thing that's important is that you be consistent throughout your resume. It's a small detail, yes, but every little touch of professionalism counts.

## Part 1: The Chronological Resume

# 1. The name header

**Treatment:** The name header, which tells employers who you are and how to reach you, is always the first thing on the resume page. Put the name header, or your name only, in boldface type to make it even more prominent.

**Construction:** Your name header should include your full name (or first and last names and middle initial), your address and phone number. If you are living at a temporary address (as in the case of a college student living away from home), include both your temporary and future addresses and phone numbers, and indicate the dates you can be reached at each.

Use the most professional version of your name. You want to create the image of a serious, "real" adult. So use Melissa rather than Missy; Barbara rather than Babs. And even if everyone has called you "Honey" from the time you learned to talk, use your real name on your resume—be it Harriet, Henrietta, Hildegarde or whatever.

If you have an unusual or difficult-to-pronounce name, you may want to include a pronunciation guide. This will make employers more comfortable when contacting you. For example:

*Julia Kjell*
*(pronounced "shell")*

Wait! Given the possibility of gender discrimination, could it be advantageous to conceal the fact that you are a woman? Should you deliberately avoid indicating your gender—say, by using just your initials instead of your full name?

The experts say no. Absolutely not. Don't make sex an issue. If employers are so blatantly biased as to eliminate all women from the job-search process, changing your name on your resume isn't going to help you get the job—they're going to figure out sooner or later that you're a woman, after all. And employers who aren't discriminatory may feel a bit conned, which could hurt your chances as well.

## Dressing up your address

Some resume guides advise "doctoring" your address—for instance, indicating that you live in a major city as opposed to an outlying suburb. Such tactics not only aren't worth the fuss, they can be downright dangerous. Unless you give your correct address, employers may not be able to contact you!

## Telephone tag: the kiss of death

The phone number is the most crucial and most problematic element in the name header. You need to list a number where prospective employers can reach you during hours that *they* are working. This creates difficulties if you are currently working during those very same hours. Unless you answer your own phone or otherwise run no risks if a potential employer contacts you at work, you shouldn't include your work number.

Of course, you can't expect employers to contact you at home after business hours, either. The solution? Put your home phone number on your resume, then buy, beg, rent or borrow an answering machine if you don't already own one. Another option is to sign up for the voice mail services your phone company may offer. Whatever you do, don't rely on someone else living in your home to take your messages.

Make sure that the outgoing message on your answering machine sounds professional and states your full name—not just your first name or your phone number. People are often hesitant to leave a message unless they know for sure they've reached the right person. And no joke messages, no messages from your cat or your kids. Check for messages frequently and return any calls immediately.

# 2. The job objective (optional)

**Treatment:** If you decide to use one, the job objective should appear first on the resume, directly after the name header. Set off the objective with the headline "Objective," "Job Objective" or "Career Objective."

**Construction:** Somewhere along the line, it became popular to use vague, wishy-washy objectives that read something like:

> *To utilize my skills and talents in a position with a forward-thinking company that allows me to contribute to the success of the company and grow in my career.*

However, if you use an objective like that today, you'll only waste time and precious resume space. It tells the employer nothing, and it certainly doesn't paint the picture of someone who knows what she wants out of life.

Instead, state exactly what type of position you seek. You want to avoid the "I'm anybody you want me to be" approach. Your objective should communicate, "This is who I am. This is what I want to do." Be strong, confident, focused—and concise. Limit yourself to 10 or 12 words. Here are two examples:

*Inside sales position for a telecommunications company.*

*Women's apparel buyer for a department store.*

## 3. The skills summary (optional)

The skills summary, which is a brief roundup of your qualifications, also must be succinctly stated and targeted to your job goal. Your summary should highlight experience and qualifications most relevant to the position you want. Stick with specific experience, skills and training; don't include references to personal work habits, such as "hard-working," "loyal," etc.

**Treatment:** If you use a summary, it should appear directly after your name header or the job objective, if you include that element. Headline choices include "Skills Summary," "Experience Summary," and "Summary of Qualifications." You can write your summary in paragraph style or as a list of bulleted points.

**Construction:** Your goal is to write a summary that makes the employer stop and think, "Aha! Here's exactly the kind of experience we're looking for. I want to read on."

If you use the paragraph style, limit yourself to two or three short sentences. Here are two examples:

*Registered dietitian with eight years clinical experience in a hospital setting. Master's degree in adult education; two years university teaching experience.*

*Five years experience as a systems programmer/analyst for major international corporations. Proficient in COBOL, C and FOCUS programming languages. Special expertise in marketing-support systems.*

If you choose the bullet-listing style, include just four or five bulleted points. An example:

- *10 years professional advertising design experience.*
- *Winner of 5 ADDY awards.*
- *Expertise in Adobe Illustrator, PageMaker and other desktop publishing software.*
- *Strong background in banking, real estate and telecommunications advertising.*

If you're not sure what to include, you may want to go ahead and complete the rest of your resume. Reviewing the sum total of your experience and qualifications should help you develop your skills summary. Or, refer back to your worksheets, especially the "Skills Summary" page, or consult your Career Card file.

Remember, *always put your most important and most relevant qualifications first in your summary!* If you are pursuing two different career directions and creating two resumes, you'll have to alter your summary to match each goal.

# 4. Experience

In this section—the backbone of your resume—you'll detail your work experience and accomplishments.

Note that when we say "work experience," we are not necessarily referring to paid work experience. For matters of convenience, we'll refer to volunteer experience and paid experience jointly as "experience" throughout this section.

**Treatment:** Depending on your situation, you may want to:

**1. List paid and volunteer positions separately.** Create two listings of your positions, labeling one "Employment History" or "Professional Experience" (to indicate that jobs detailed were paid positions) and the other "Volunteer Experience," "Other Experience," or "Related Experience."

One section should follow immediately after the other. Which listing you put first—and how much emphasis you give to each—depends on which experience is most relevant to your job goal.

**2. Combine volunteer and paid positions into one chronological listing.** This can be very effective when both types of experience are relevant to your goals or when combining the two closes career gaps. A good heading for a section including both types of experience is, "Professional and Volunteer Experience" or simply, "Experience."

However, if you've held down volunteer and paid positions simultaneously, this format can get a little confusing; employers may have a difficult time sorting out the timeline of your career. In this case, it's probably best to separate the two types of experience into two listings. Ditto if your volunteer experience is very different in nature from your paid experience—for example, if you're employed as a physical therapist but your volunteer experience is in the cultural arts arena.

**3. List paid positions only.** If your volunteer experience isn't particularly noteworthy or relevant to your job goal, you can simply mention your involvement at the end of the resume, in your memberships and activities section.

In a moment, we'll discuss each of the components of the experience profile in depth. But first, let's look at how those components might be combined on the page. A classic style for presenting your experience is demonstrated below:

---

1989-1993     **Shangri-La Hotels, Inc.,** New York City
              **Promotions Manager**
              Developed image and marketing campaign to
              promote national hotel chain. Supervised
              staff of seven designers, copywriters and
              marketing specialists.
              - Increased database of qualified prospects by
                50%.
              - Designed promotion that increased annual
                net profit by 5%.
              - Created ad campaigns that won travel-
                industry awards.

---

If you've had several different positions at one company—especially if you've been promoted—that's a plus. It shows that you're a loyal employee and that you're capable of handling increased levels of responsibility. To avoid repeating the employer's name before each position and to emphasize that you stayed in one place for a number of years, you might want to list your positions as shown on the following page. Notice how specific dates for each position are included after the job title.

1985-present     **ABC Manufacturing Company,** Bryan, Wisconsin

**Sales Manager,** 1990 to present. Direct sales activities of 15 regional sales representatives serving the Eastern U.S.
- Exceeded company sales goals on a reduced budget.
- Created "Preferred Client" program that increased orders from key customers while maintaining appropriate profit levels.

**Sales Associate,** 1987 to 1990. Sold industrialized widgets to manufacturing corporations throughout Pennsylvania. Developed and maintained 300-company client base.
- Acquired 15 major new corporate clients during a two-year period.

**Sales Support Coordinator,** 1985 to 1987. Provided administrative support to five regional sales representatives.
- Developed centralized sales-accounting system that generated more accurate sales reports and reduced paperwork.

Construction: In the chronological format, you list your most recent position first and work backwards through your career history. Usually, the first few listings in your profile will contain more information than the last few; presumably, you would have more accomplishments to relate in your most recent positions than you would have for jobs you had earlier in life, when you had less experience and fewer responsibilities.

The exact content of the individual listings of your experience profile will depend upon the importance of each position. Your most recent and most relevant positions should include the following:

1. Name of employer.
2. Employer's location.
3. Your dates of employment or affiliation.
4. Your position or job title.
5. A summary of your responsibilities.
6. Your major accomplishments.

Include this "full" listing for the first four to six positions in your profile or for the first seven to 10 years of your experience. After that, detail positions in full only if doing so lends additional strength to your resume. Otherwise, just state the employer's name and location, your position and dates of employment.

Now, let's get into the nitty-gritty of writing your experience listings. Here's how to handle each element of a full listing.

**1. Employer or organization name and location.** State the company's full name, along with location, unless that is obvious from the employer's name.

When listing the name of an organization that is known by a nickname or its initials that may be unfamiliar to employers, give the full name first, followed by the initials in parentheses. For example: "Michaelson Tire and Tool (MTT)." It's okay to refer to the organization thereafter by the initials.

**2. Work timeline.** Indicate the month and year you began and left each position. If you've been in the work force many years, and you were at each job for a year or more, you can consider dropping the month.

**3. Your job title.** If your actual job title wasn't very glamorous or you did more than your title reflects, you may be tempted to "alter" it just a bit. For example, suppose you were hired as an administrative assistant to a meeting planner, but you actually did most of the meeting planning work. Should you put down "meeting planner" as your job title?

Proceed with caution! What would happen if a prospective employer called your former boss to verify that you were employed as a meeting planner? Don't run the risk of being caught in what might be perceived as a lie.

Many companies have rigid title hierarchies. If you change your title from "creative projects coordinator" to "creative director," you may offend and anger the person your prospective employer contacts to verify your position. Never improve the status of your position by listing a title that implies you were higher up on the company ladder than you actually were.

However, it's probably okay to make *slight* changes in your title. If first-line supervisors in your company were referred to as "group leaders," you should be safe using the more universally understood title, "supervisor." It wouldn't hurt to alert your former boss that you've done this, if possible, so that he or she won't be caught off guard if asked about it.

**4. A brief description of your responsibilities.** Keep this short—just one or two brief statements. Remember, your resume is a selling tool, not a job description. Don't try to mention every function; sum up your major responsibilities in broad terms. You can state your summary in paragraph form, or combine it with your accomplishments in one list of bulleted points.

Indicate your level of responsibility—the size of the budget you controlled, the number of people you supervised, the amount of revenue you were responsible for, and so on. Although you shouldn't try to mislead employers into thinking your job was something it was not, focus on those responsibilities most relevant to your new job goal.

When summarizing your responsibilities, use action words. Avoid using the same words; don't begin every statement with "Directed," for example. To give you help in this area, see the list on page 111.

**5. A list of your most important or relevant accomplishments.** List a few accomplishments that show that you were successful in your position. State your accomplishments in specific terms, including the amount of revenue saved or earned, if relevant.

Refer to your worksheets and career file for details. If you have many accomplishments, select those that will be the most impressive given the type of job you are seeking. Ask yourself when writing your accomplishments, does this point reflect:

- How I increased profits?
- How I saved the company money?
- How I solved problems?
- How I increased efficiency or productivity?
- How I met or exceeded goals?

Because this is often a problem area for resume writers, let's review a few examples of accomplishments.

**Example #1:** Suppose you're in corporate accounting and one of your duties is to coordinate the annual budgeting process for three key departments. But each year, yours is the only division that completes budgets ahead of schedule. This says that you not only do what you are supposed to do, but that you go above and beyond the call of duty. Your accomplishment statement must reflects that fact.

Before
- *Coordinated annual budgeting process for three departments.*

After
- *Coordinated development of $15 million annual budget for three key departments; only budget unit consistently completed ahead of schedule.*

# Action words to use in your resume

| | | |
|---|---|---|
| accomplished | distributed | performed |
| achieved | edited | persuaded |
| adjusted | eliminated | planned |
| administered | enlarged | prepared |
| advised | established | presented |
| analyzed | evaluated | processed |
| approved | examined | produced |
| arranged | expanded | promoted |
| assisted | formulated | proposed |
| built | founded | provided |
| calculated | guided | purchased |
| charted | headed | recommended |
| compared | identified | reduced |
| compiled | implemented | referred |
| completed | improved | reorganized |
| composed | increased | replaced |
| conducted | initiated | reported |
| consolidated | inspected | represented |
| constructed | installed | researched |
| consulted | instituted | restored |
| controlled | instructed | reviewed |
| coordinated | interpreted | revised |
| counseled | invented | scheduled |
| created | justified | selected |
| decreased | led | served |
| delivered | lectured | sold |
| designated | made | solved |
| designed | maintained | studied |
| detected | managed | supervised |
| determined | modified | supplied |
| developed | motivated | taught |
| devised | negotiated | tested |
| diagnosed | obtained | trained |
| directed | operated | translated |
| discovered | ordered | won |
| disproved | organized | wrote |

**Example #2:** You've been membership chairman of a civic association for three years. Your duties are to enroll new members and maintain existing memberships. Each year, you have exceeded enrollment goals by 50 percent, and you've increased your member-retention rate from 70 percent to 85 percent. In other words, you've done a great job! See how the "before" statement downplays your accomplishments, while the "after" statement makes it clear that you're not only capable of meeting goals, but have the drive and wits to surpass them.

Before
- *Enroll new members and maintain existing memberships.*

After
- *Exceeded member enrollment goals by 50% for three years in a row.*
- *Increased member-retention rate by 15% over a three-year period.*

**Example #3:** Sometimes, what you did is not so important as the conditions under which you did it. For example, remember Sandra's sample resume (Chapter 9, Case Study #5)? One of her accomplishments was acquiring 400 new YWCA members in a one-year period. That's impressive. It's even more impressive when you know that she accomplished this during the initial development stage of the YWCA. There were no facilities or programs for members to enjoy yet—members got absolutely nothing in return for their membership fee except a good feeling about being a "charter member." The "before" accomplishment statement below is okay, but the "after" has much more impact, because it illustrates that Sandra succeeds despite hurdles in her path.

Before
- *Conceived and organized marketing campaigns that resulted in 400 new members in a one-year period.*

After
- *Conceived and organized marketing campaigns that resulted in 400 new members in a one-year period. Members acquired during this time received no services in exchange for membership fees (YWCA facilities not yet built).*

# 5. Education

**Treatment:** Details about your education generally follow the experience section in both the chronological and functional resume.

However, there are some situations when it makes sense for this information to appear first:

1. You're a recent college graduate with little experience.
2. You're changing careers, and your education is more pertinent to your new area of interest than your recent job experience.
3. You're seeking a job in a field where specialized education is a prerequisite for employment.

**Construction:** You need only provide basic details about your education unless you have no volunteer or paid work experience, in which case your education is your only marketable commodity. (More about that scenario in a moment.) Otherwise, just include:

1. The name and location of the school (city and state unless either are evident from the name).
2. The date of your graduation.
3. Your degree or major area of study.
4. Your GPA (optional).

## Post-secondary education

When listing college and trade-school degrees, you can use the abbreviated forms B.A., B.S., M.B.A., etc.—or spell out the degree name: Bachelor of Science degree, etc. Whichever form you choose, be consistent throughout all listings.

Like all of the other elements of your resume, the specific arrangement of your post-high school education depends upon what you believe to be the most impressive to prospective employers. The placement of the degree you earned, the school you attended and the years of your attendance can be shifted about to put emphasis on one aspect or detract from another.

If you want to emphasize the school you attended rather than the degree you earned or courses you took, for example, you would list the school name first:

*Harvard University, Cambridge, Massachusetts; B.S. in General Business, 1990*

On the other hand, if you feel your degree would be a better sales point than your alma mater, put your degree first:

*B.S. in Economics, 1980, State College, Grandview, Oregon*

If you have more than one degree, list the most recent or relevant first. If you graduated with honors, you can note that fact in your "Honors and Awards" section or within your educational listing:

*B.S., Engineering, 1987 cum laude graduate, Ohio State University, Columbus*

If you did not graduate, indicate the years that you attended instead of a graduation date. If you completed many credit hours, be sure to state the numbers. Here's an effective way to treat this information:

*Arizona University, Tucson, computer programming courses, 1989-1991*

*University of Southern California, Los Angeles, 30 credit hours in computer science, 1976-1978*

Notice how these listings de-emphasize dates while playing up the school and area of course work. (Getting the hang of this "best foot forward" thing now?)

If you have specific course work related to your job goal, but that course work is not obvious from your degree, you can briefly indicate that fact here. For example, suppose you have a degree in business, but you took a lot of courses in film production as electives. Now you're seeking a job as a financial manager for a film-production company. Let employers know about your general knowledge of the film world:

*B.A., Business, 1984, University of Miami, Coral Gables, Florida*
*• 15 credit hours in film production and film studies.*

## High school education

Include information about your high school education only if you are a recent graduate or did not attend college or a trade school. In other words, if it is the most important educational credential that you have. If you did not graduate from high school, but later earned a GED (equivalency degree), provide that information instead.

If you attended several different high schools, list the one you last attended or from which you received a diploma. Include the same pieces of information as you would for a college degree, except the area of study:

*Wabash High School, Wabash, Texas, graduated May 1986*

Should you include high school data after you've long since put away your yearbook? Probably not, even if that is your only formal education. It's simply not very relevant to employers. And you're in a no-win situation when it comes to providing the date of your high-school years: Tell an employer that you graduated from high school in 1959, and you've announced your age, loud and clear. Leave off the date, and employers may suspect that you're trying to hide your age. Either way, age discrimination may rear its illegal, but nonetheless prevalent, head.

So if your high school years are as much a part of the past as poodle skirts, love beads and even disco balls, don't mention them on your resume.

## Should you include GPA?

If you've been in the work force for many years—say, 10 to 20—there's no need to include information about your grades in school. Your accomplishments and experience should be enough to indicate that you are intelligent and hard-working. If your grades were truly exceptional, of course, you won't do yourself any harm in mentioning your GPA (grade point average), unless doing so takes up page space you might fill with more recent accomplishments.

But whether you've been out of school for decades or just a month or so, list your GPA only if you had good grades! As a general rule of thumb, include your GPA if it was 3.5 or higher on a 4.0 scale, or 5.0 and up on a 6.0 scale. Be sure to provide both your GPA and the scale on which it was registered.

Alternatively, you can list your class ranking, if that's more impressive. If you graduated with honors, and you mention that in your degree listing, there's no need to add your GPA—your educational prowess is already implied.

You can indicate your grade average or ranking as follows:

*B.A., Music Education, 1991, Howard University,*
*Washington, D.C., 3.7/4.0 GPA*

*Brown High School, Jasper, N.H.*
*Graduated May 1990; ranked 5th in class of 250*

## Special educational experiences

You may want to mention any unique educational experience you've had, such as spending a year as a foreign exchange student. Even if these experiences aren't directly linked to your career goal, they indicate that you are a person who goes one step beyond the norm, who's open to new opportunities and challenges.

For example, suppose you studied art in Paris during your junior year in college. Include it in a bulleted point after you list your degree, as so:

*B.A., Art History, 1979,*
*Drake University, Des Moines, Iowa*
• *One year of foreign study in Paris, at Parisian Art Institute.*

Another experience worth mentioning is an internship. If you prefer, you can profile internship experience as you would a regular paid or volunteer position in your Experience section. Otherwise, you can detail it like so:

*B.A., Radio-TV-Film, 1984, Northwestern University,*
*Evanston, Ill.*
• *One-year film production internship at Chicago Film Board.*

## Expanded educational listings

If you're just out of school and have little work experience, you'll need to play up your educational experience in much greater detail than outlined above. You can include:

1. Course work related to your job objective.
2. School activities.
3. Educational accomplishments.

As much as possible, present this information in the same format as you would professional experience—that is, focusing on specific accomplishments. For a look at how to format this information, review Kristen's resume, (Case Study #3 in Chapter 9), and the instructions given in the education worksheet in Chapter 4.

# 6. Licensing, certification and special training

**Treatment:** List any special training you've had and any professional licenses or certification you currently hold. Use whatever heading is appropriate: "Training and Certification," "Professional Licenses," "Special Training," etc. If you prefer, you can group this information together with your education information instead of making it a separate section.

**Construction:** For professional licenses and certification, include:

1. Name and type of license.
2. The state or states in which it is valid, if appropriate.

3. The date it was acquired.

4. Number of the license, if appropriate.

Here are some examples:

- *Ohio Teaching Certification, elementary education, 1980.*
- *Montana Real Estate License, 1991.*
- *Certified Public Accountant, New Jersey, 1988.*

For special training, include:

1. Name of the course.

2. Name and location of the institution where you took the course.

3. The date you completed the training.

If the skills you profile in this section will be vital in your new job, this treatment is okay only if you are putting your Education and Training information at the top of the resume. Otherwise, you're missing the boat, because you're lessening the prominence of this data.

A better option is to weave it into your experience profile—ideally, within your accomplishments. This will indicate that you not only were trained in these skills, but also used them on a daily basis and, in the case of related accomplishments, that you excelled in them. Another alternative is to include this information in a skills summary at the top of the resume.

## Company-paid seminars?

Especially in corporate life, most employers routinely send employees to professional development seminars. These one-day or one-week seminars typically deal with such subjects as how to communicate better with co-workers, how to manage staff members, and other aspects of business interaction. This kind of special training, while it can certainly be valuable, is not "resume worthy." Your attendance or completion of such courses does not indicate a major accomplishment because rarely is any major effort on the part of trainees required.

However, if you completed a special training program that is more akin to a regular college or trade-school course, and it is related to your career, go ahead and mention it. A good example is an extensive training course on a particular type of computer software. Here's how you might state this data:

- *Desktop publishing: Completed intensive, three-month training program; Wright Computer Systems Training Center; Lincoln, Nebraska, May 1990.*

# 7. Memberships and activities

**Treatment:** This is the place for mentioning any memberships and activities you did not previously detail in your main experience profile.

The title you give this section should, like others in your resume, reflect its contents. If you list only professional affiliations, title the section "Professional Affiliations." If you list only community organizations, title the section "Community Activities" or "Outside Activities."

Affiliations you mention here don't necessarily need to be related to your career. The goal of this section is simply to let employers know that you are a good citizen, a well-rounded individual and—especially impressive in these busy, harried times—that you can manage your time well enough to permit involvement in outside activities!

However, if you belong to lots of professional and social organizations, include only a handful of those that will be most meaningful to prospective employers. Affiliations related to your career and organizations in which you have made significant contributions should be given priority.

**Construction:** Unlike volunteer positions you chronicle in your experience profile, all the activities you mention in this section should be current activities. No filling up the page with memberships you let expire 10 years ago. Keep listings brief, mentioning just the name of the organization and any leadership position you hold.

Consider carefully what you choose to include. Membership in organizations that provide community or school support are all relatively safe. But a mention of your involvement with a certain political party, religious group or controversial organizations such as NOW and Planned Parenthood could set off silent alarms of discrimination.

Here are some sample listings:

- *Board of Directors, Earth Day Cincinnati, 1990-present.*

- *Member, Greater Cincinnati Businesswoman's Association.*

- *Member, Spartan High School PTA, Cincinnati; Membership chair, 1989-1990.*

If you want, you can include an accomplishment—but if it's a significant accomplishment, or you have lots of accomplishments to mention, better to move all of this information into your main experience or volunteer section. You want to spotlight such experience, and because a memberships and activities section might not get more than a glance from employers, this isn't the place to do it.

# 8. Awards and honors

**Treatment:** Awards and honors you received as a result of work experience, of course, should already be included as accomplishments within your experience profile. Why there, and not here? Because this section usually falls near the end of the resume—and you want your career-related awards to have more prominence.

If you do, in fact, have honors and awards to mention in your experience profile, be sure to title this section "Additional Awards and Honors" or "Other Honors and Awards," so that employers are reminded that these are not your only special achievements. Otherwise, the title "Awards and Honors" will do fine.

**Construction:** List only significant honors that will reinforce the impression that you are an outstanding citizen, an exceptional student or a specially talented and motivated individual. ("Best Holiday Lawn Decoration" is an example of what *not* to include—unless, of course, you want a job as a lawn decorator.)

Provide the name of the award, the organization that awarded it, and then the year in which you received it. If it's not obvious from the title of the award, include information that will tell the employer why you were honored. Include only those honors you've won in the past five years—unless, it's some remarkable recognition of national significance.

Some examples of how to list these individual awards:

- *Phi Beta Kappa, elected to membership 1992.*
- *National Merit Scholarship Winner, 1991.*
- *Tri-County Triathlon Winner, Austin, Georgia, 1993.*

# 9. Hobbies and outside interests

If you include it, this section should always appear last on your resume—it's the least important of your qualifications. Keep it short and simple; generally, one line will do:

*Running, community theater, photography*

Remember that you'll do better to list those hobbies likely to be perceived as potential additional benefits you can offer employers. And, as with social and professional affiliations, avoid mentioning controversial hobbies; your fixation with taxidermy or the occult probably won't win you any employment points.

---

# Part II: The Functional Resume

---

Most elements in a functional resume are handled in the same manner as in a chronological resume, except for work experience and accomplishments. Instead of presenting a year-by-year accounting of your work whereabouts, you provide a listing of your experiences and accomplishments according to area of skill. Here's the basic recipe for putting together this kind of resume.

## 1. The name header

Follow the same instructions as for a chronological resume.

## 2. The job objective and skills summary

Because employers may have a difficult time discerning your job goal from a functional resume, it's appropriate in most cases to include a job objective or skills summary.

Choose a job objective if you know precisely what type of job you want, and if you are not interested in any other position. Write your objective according to the instructions given for the chronological resume.

If you opt to include a skills summary, provide a one- or two-sentence statement that sums up your most important qualifications for the position you seek. The strongest summaries include the number of years experience you have in particular areas you choose to highlight. If you don't have years of experience, you can simply say, "Strong background in..." or "Extensive experience in..."

To write your summary, refer to the rules explained earlier, in the chronological format section of this chapter.

## 3. The skill and experience profile

**Treatment:** Here's where the chronological and functional formats diverge. Don't list each position you have held, including responsibilities and accomplishments related to each.

---

Instead, divide your experience profile into general areas of skill, and briefly state experience, qualifications and accomplishments related to each of those areas.

**Construction:** The first step is to decide what skill categories you will highlight. To do that, think about what skills would be most needed in the position you're seeking.

For example, suppose you're applying for a job as a supervisor at a day-care center. What general areas of expertise would be most important? Childcare, teaching, management and general business come to mind. Ideally, you would have at least some experience, qualifications and accomplishments to list in each of these areas. That experience might come from a combination of paid jobs, volunteer positions and in-the-home responsibilities.

Under each skills-category heading, you should list four or five of your most impressive experiences or accomplishments.

Following is an example of how a portion of this resume might look on the page. Because childcare experience would be the most important qualification for this job, it is listed first on the resume, followed by management experience, which would be the second most important.

### Childcare experience

- *Provided in-home day care for three preschoolers for two years.*
- *Assisted with toddler care in corporate day-care center.*
- *Cared for infants in a church nursery for two years.*
- *Developed "child file" system that made vital medical data on day-care children easier to access and maintain.*
- *Raised three children.*

### Management experience

- *Supervised three cashiers as first-line supervisor in large discount store.*
- *Created employee scheduling procedure that resolved long-standing staffing conflicts.*
- *Named Employee of the Month for designing and implementing improved inventory-return system.*
- *Coordinated and directed activities of 100 PTA volunteers for annual fund-raising dinner for three years.*

Notice how the bulleted points are a mix of experience statements and accomplishments. If you have more than one year of experience in any one area, you should highlight that by stating the specific number of years, as in the first bullet point under "Childcare Experience."

### Experience timeline

According to some resume books, a "pure" functional resume does not include mention of the specific dates of your employment or work in volunteer groups. Some books say that it's even okay to leave off the names of employers. We, however, recommend otherwise.

These pieces of information are important to employers. If you leave them off, you're going to raise suspicions. The employer's reasoning is, "Why would someone not mention those details unless she wanted to hide something?" You likely will be rejected from consideration on this basis alone.

The most effective functional resume includes a brief work experience profile stating your employment and volunteer history in chronological fashion. You don't have to emphasize this information—but you should include it.

It can be something as brief and simple as the following:

### Work history

- *Community volunteer and homemaker, Goshen, Georgia, 1990-present.*
- *Infant-care provider, All Saints Church, Goshen, Georgia, 1989-present.*
- *In-home day-care provider, Bethesda, Georgia, 1987-1989.*
- *Greenbriar Elementary School PTA Fund raising committee, Bethesda, Georgia, 1987-1989.*
- *Head cashier, Brown's Handi Mart, Bethesda, Georgia, 1984-1986.*

# 4. Other Elements

All other elements of the resume, including education, special training, honors and awards, etc., should be written in the same manner described earlier in this chapter under "Creating the Chronological Resume."

# Resume Q & A

In the years since this book was first published, we've fielded all sorts of resume questions at workshops and seminars, and on radio and TV talk shows. A few questions seem to pop up over and over again—such as how to avoid looking like a job-hopper, for example, and whether it's a good idea to specify whether experience was obtained in a paid or volunteer position. (Interestingly, the one question that *doesn't* pop up a lot is, "Where can I buy 10 copies of your book?")

We expect that you may share some of the same concerns as those who call us for advice. So the remainder of this chapter answers some common questions that haven't already been addressed in earlier sections.

*I've grouped my volunteer experience and professional experience together under one heading, "Experience." Should I indicate which experience was paid, and which wasn't?*

Some career counselors say this isn't necessary because it's irrelevant whether you were paid—experience is experience, and volunteer experience is as worthy of credit as a paid position. Most employers would agree. Still, if you believe prospective employers may feel that you've misled them in any way, it's best to indicate which was which.

*I've spent several years at home with my kids. Should I list "Domestic Engineer" as a job?*

No. Although you needn't hide the fact that you were a mother and homemaker, neither should you dress it up with coy pseudo-titles. Employers may feel duped once they understand the real nature of your experience. If you don't have enough paid or volunteer experience to list actual positions in a chronological format, consider a functional format. That way, you can focus on the skills you have without emphasizing the fact that you acquired them in the home.

*Should I mention why I left each position?*

Not on your resume. It's not considered standard resume fare, and if you do include this information, you'll only raise questions or get yourself eliminated. It may be an issue you'll be asked to address in interviews; see Chapter 16 for some appropriate ways to handle it.

*When I started out, it took me a few years and a half-dozen jobs before I decided where I really belong. I spent only a few months on some jobs. How do I avoid looking like a job-hopper?*

If you have 10 years or more of a stable work history, you can simply leave off those "ancient" jobs or de-emphasize them by listing just the employer's name, your title and the dates of your employment. Leave off a description of your job and your accomplishments, and use the space you save to focus on more recent and more relevant positions.

However, if you don't have years of experience...be truthful, and list all of your various positions. As much as possible, focus on responsibilities related to your current job goal. And do include an accomplishment for each position. It's important for employers to know that even though you only stayed a few months, you made a valuable contribution. In interviews and in your cover letter, you can combat any negative impressions related to your job-hopping by saying that your early career exploration: 1) gave you a broad business background; and 2) helped you determine that your true calling was in your current field.

Whatever you do, don't lie. Your credibility is one of the most valuable things you have to sell, and you'll destroy it if you're less than truthful.

*Every time I sit down to write my resume, I just can't seem to get started. Help!*

Every resume writer—every writer, for that matter—goes through some form of writer's block. There's nothing like looking at a blank sheet of paper to make you want to leave the room, fast.

To get beyond "write fright," make a deal with yourself to write *something* for at least one hour. Put down whatever comes to mind, and don't criticize yourself as you go. At the end of your one hour, you'll be surprised at the dent you've made in your resume. And because starting is always the hardest part of writing, the rest will all be downhill from there.

Remember, too, that you are only writing a rough draft at this point—so don't expect or demand perfection of yourself. When you've got your rough draft completed, you'll be ready to move on to the next chapter, where we'll help you polish that rough gem into a dazzling marketing jewel.

# Chapter 11

# Design Strategies: Resume Do's and Don'ts

A popular women's magazine publishes a regular feature in which hapless fashion victims are offered up to the world as "don'ts"—as in, "don't be caught dead dressed like this."

Having been raised in the suburban Midwest, where fashion trends appear long after they've been announced in Paris, we often had a difficult time figuring out exactly what was so "don't" about some of the outfits pictured. Many flaws, of course, were obvious—even we knew you shouldn't wear a slip that hung beneath the hem of your dress. But others were more subtle. There'd be a shot of a woman in some ensemble that looked fine to our untrained eyes (in fact, we had similar get-ups in our own closets). It was only after reading the explanatory caption that we learned that the outfit was a no-no because its cut didn't complement that particular woman.

The story is much the same when it comes to the do's and don'ts of resume design. As in fashion, there are some obvious pitfalls that, if not avoided, can ruin an otherwise splendid resume. And just as you can use different shades and styles of clothing to play up your best physical features, you can employ various design strategies to emphasize your most impressive job qualifications.

In this chapter, we'll review the rules of resume design, discussing such issues as type size and style, margins and page layout. You'll learn how to incorporate these different elements into your resume in a way that not only creates an attractive first impression, but strengthens your marketing impact.

## Trademarks of a well-dressed resume

- Easy to read.
- Lots of white space.
- Neat.
- Clean.

Those four design characteristics were mentioned most often when we asked employment experts to tell us what a resume should look like. The words *conservative*, *sophisticated*, *powerful* and *professional* also came up repeatedly.

It all boils down to the old 30-second rule—the average time limit that employers will spend screening a resume. To make the most of your 30 seconds, you must:

1. **Make your resume easy and inviting to read.** It should look simple and uncluttered, with type and white space arranged so that the reader's eye is drawn quickly from beginning to end.

2. **Use traditional type and layouts.** One glance at your resume should tell employers that you are a serious professional, well-versed in the conventions of business communication.

3. **Spotlight your most important sales points.** Your most impressive and relevant qualifications must be highlighted with boldface type or other design elements so that they will be immediately apparent to someone scanning your resume.

Perhaps the most important design rule is that your resume should *look* like a resume! We've heard of resumes presented on the backs of milk cartons. Slipped inside fortune cookies. Printed on business cards and recorded on video, complete with a musical score. Friends who work in a corporate HR department still talk about the resume delivered by the singing gorilla and the one stapled to the lid of a pizza box (which included a large deep-dish with pepperoni and mushrooms, compliments of the sender).

Memorable, they are. And some are certainly strong contenders for the "Most Creative Resume" award. Yet, these job-seekers failed to win the biggest prize of all—the job.

Fun is fun, but when employers are about to invest time and money in a new employee, they tend to be straightforward and serious. So don't resort to gimmicks. They simply don't work.

## What about the "creative fields"?

You've probably heard that if you're in a creative profession, such as writing, art, theater or graphic design, it pays to spice up your resume with some "fun" elements that illustrate your talent. Well, we're not going to tell you that this approach never works. A woman in the interior design business has on her resume a graphic reproduction of a woven textile. She's been using this device since graduation from college 10 years ago—and she's landed every job she's ever gone after.

If you think such an element might be appropriate for you, use the utmost caution. Test out your idea on lots of friends, peers and professional acquaintances; if any one of them indicates that you might not be taken seriously, deep-six your creative impulse. And never let graphic devices become so large or powerful that they detract from your professional qualifications.

As a rule, you're safer to play it straight with your resume and save the creative dazzle for your portfolio. This demonstrates that you can be both imaginative and businesslike.

# 20 Tips for better-looking (and more effective) resumes

Looks aren't everything, but in the case of your resume, they are critical. Design decisions can make or break your sales presentation. So when you're fashioning your resume look, remember the following 20 rules of effective resume design.

**1. Keep your resume to one or two pages.** In past years, the experts insisted that a resume should never exceed one page. This is no longer a valid rule. Today, one- and two-page resumes are acceptable.

Employers recognize that if you've been in the work force for several years and have accumulated a variety of valuable experiences and skills, you need two pages to describe them adequately. So don't sell yourself short by cutting out impressive qualifications just to squeeze your resume on one page. But it should be longer than two pages.

**2. Don't crowd** three pages worth of information onto two pages by reducing type size, shrinking margins and eliminating spacing. If pages are too full, you need to go back to the drawing board and cut excess data.

**3. If your resume continues to a second page,** add the word "continued" at the bottom of the first page, and put your name and the words "page 2" at the top of the second page. In a stack of resumes on a busy employer's desk, your pages might become separated.

**4. Use a serif typeface** rather than sans serif type. The difference? Serif types—such as the New Century Schoolbook used in this book—have extra little strokes on their letters—little hats and tails on their abc's. Sans serifs, on the other hand, are unembellished, plain faces, such as the example below.

Helvetica is a sans serif typeface

The serifs help pull the eye more quickly and easily through the page, improving readability. Sounds a little crazy, we know, but there are people out there who study these things, and they have proven this to be true.

**5. Save fancy script typefaces for wedding invitations** and birth announcements. Resist the urge to try out those artsy, 3-D shaded letters. Stick to traditional typefaces such as Bookman, Times New Roman, New Century Schoolbook or Souvenir.

**6. Choose a readable size.** Body type (everything but the name header and section heads) should be 10- or 12-point type. Never go smaller than 10-point type. You may want to make the name header and section headings a little larger for emphasis—generally, one or two point sizes up from body type is appropriate.

**7. Don't mix typefaces.** For example, don't use Century School-book in one part of your resume and Souvenir in another. Stay with one typeface throughout.

**8. Highlight with boldface type.** By making some words darker and heavier than others (as we've done with the headlines in this book), you draw the reader's eye to them. Typically, you'll want to boldface such data as your name, job titles, the names of employers and your degrees. Of course, you'll only boldface those elements you want to emphasize in the reader's mind—if you want to play up your job title and not the employer who gave you that title, leave the employer's name in regular weight type. Be sparing with this technique—use too much bold type, and you dilute its effect.

**9. Use all-cap and underlining treatments sparingly,** perhaps just for section heads:

SKILLS SUMMARY or
<u>Skills Summary</u>

**10. Don't underline words or phrases or use all caps in body copy.** Research shows that both treatments slow and even stop the eye from reading. They are best reserved for your name and for section heads.

**11. Use italic type sparingly.** In books and magazine articles, italic type is often used to *emphasize* a word or phrase. In a well-written resume, which presents information in short, punchy phrases, there is no need for this sort of emphasis. Never set your whole resume in italic type; it's too hard to read. An example of when italic type might be appropriate is seen in Sandra's revised resume (Case Study #5, Chapter 9). Here, it's used to separate blocks of employment without drawing undue emphasis to the employers' names.

**12. Be generous with margins.** Leave at least one inch at the top of the page, and ideally, use one-inch margins around the other three borders as well. Never go smaller than a half-inch margin. Large margins create a pleasing, organized, uncluttered feeling. And on a practical side, many employers like to make notes in the margins.

**13. Use "ragged right" type layout.** In other words, let lines break naturally, instead of "justifying" copy so that all lines end at exactly the same point at the right margin. The box-like effect created by justified copy is too formal and often eats up needed white space.

> This paragraph is set in ragged right style. The words are spaced normally and not hyphenated, so the lines break unevenly along the right margin.

> This paragraph is justified. Extra spaces are inserted between words so that words are aligned evenly along the right margin.

**14. Single-space between the lines of individual listings; double-space between sections and paragraphs.** This divides information into easily digestible doses and wards off the "sea of type" look, which is intimidating and difficult to read. (*USA Today* isn't one of the most widely read papers in the country for nothing!) If you're working with a word processor, you have much more flexibility in terms of spacing than on a typewriter. You can put 2 and 1/8 lines between paragraphs, for example, or use any other line-spacing increment you choose. That's fine; just be sure that you use consistent and ample spacing throughout.

**15. Use bullets or asterisks to highlight accomplishments**. This not only breaks up a lot of information into bite-size portions, but also helps pull out key selling points that would be buried if presented in long paragraph form. See the difference in the following examples. Which one is easier to read?

**Assistant Department Manager,** Kmart. San Antonio, Texas, 1990-1991.
Supervised, scheduled and maintained sales activity in housewares department. Worked part-time during school year. First part-time employee and student promoted to this position. Directed four part-time employees. Revised merchandise layout and recommended changes that resulted in increased product visibility.

**Assistant Department Manager,** Kmart. San Antonio, Texas, 1990-1991.
Supervised, scheduled and maintained sales activity in housewares department. Worked part-time during school year.
- First part-time employee and student ever promoted to this position.
- Directed four part-time employees.
- Revised merchandise layout and recommended changes that resulted in increased product visibility.

    16. **Limit bulleted items to two or three lines of copy at the most.**

    17. **Limit paragraph length to no more than four or five lines.**

    18. **Keep line length as short as possible.** Studies have proven that it's easier to read information that's laid out in a longer block of copy with shorter lines than a short block of copy with long lines. That's because your eyes travel a shorter distance back and forth across the page. Take a look at the difference between the two examples below:

    Seven years experience as a quality-control inspector and supervisor in one of the world's largest pharmaceutical manu-facturing corporations.

        Seven years experience as a quality-control inspector and supervisor in one of the world's largest pharmaceutical manu-facturing corporations.

**19. The best way to keep line length short** is to indent all body copy about two inches from the left margin, and place only section heads and, possibly, relevant dates flush left. An effective example of indenting copy follows:

---

1988-present **Administrative Assistant**
IBM Corporation, Santa Barbara, California
- Support management staff, scheduling appointments, maintaining records and assisting with projects.
- Edited copy for and directed production of employee handbook.
- Initiated revision of supply ordering procedures, reducing costs and staff time.

1984-1988 **Secretary/Receptionist**
Jordan Corporation, Los Angeles, California
- Answered and directed telephone calls on 200-extension multiphone system.
- Trained part-time receptionists.
- Researched and implemented new telephone procedures that reduced caller hold time.

---

**20. Keep it simple!** Don't strangle your resume with a complicated design. A resume that is "overloaded" with treatments—bulging with italic type, bold type, underlined type, four or five different sizes of type, etc.—will overwhelm the reader and cause confusion. Above all, form must follow function. Your message is the most important element in your resume. The design is simply a tool to enhance it.

## Find a look that flatters

We've given you a lot of guidelines here. Yet despite the number of do's and don'ts, you really do still have room for creative flexibility. Throughout the book are sample resumes in a variety of formats. Review them, choose your favorite styles, then experiment and modify them to meet your unique circumstances.

---

# Chapter 12

# The Finishing Touches: Edit, Edit, Edit!

No one knows exactly how it got started, but somewhere in the course of time, the caricature of woman as relentless furniture rearranger was added to the list of female stereotypes. This idea has provided fodder for innumerable sitcoms, comic strips and commercials. You know the scenario: Wife wants furniture moved. Dutiful husband moves furniture as directed. Wife changes her mind. Husband moves furniture again. Wife decides everything looked better in its original arrangement. Husband moves furniture back, rolls his eyes and shares a yuk with the audience.

Of course, as with many other female stereotypes, there is a double-standard at play here. For the same man who ridicules his wife for rearranging the living room to showcase a treasured antique table is quite happy to spend hours shifting power tools and old tires so that the first thing a buddy will see upon entering the garage is the born-to-be-wild Harley Davidson in the corner.

But we digress. This particular social injustice is not the point of the story. The point is that in order to construct a really terrific resume, you must go through much the same process as you would when you are creating the perfect living room—or garage, for that matter.

## Arranging your resume for maximum impact

First, you must decide which elements belong and which do not. Then, you must play with different arrangements of those elements. And finally, you must review and refine, adding a touch here, changing an accent there, until you arrive at a setup that is perfect from both a visual and a functional standpoint.

When you wrote your rough draft, you made preliminary decisions about what pieces of information to include in your resume and how to organize those pieces on the page. Now it's time to take stock of what you've done, to review and refine.

Is there too much information? Too little? Have you chosen just the right words? Do the "accessories" you've added—the boldface type, the section heads and the like—play up your most important qualifications, or do they overpower them? Are your skills and experience arranged so that your resume not only looks good, but makes the strongest possible marketing statement? It's time to evaluate and edit, then evaluate and edit again—and again.

This process requires lots of careful thought, and it may seem tedious, especially when you're anxious to get the darned resume out in the marketplace working for you. But if ever you want to keep at it until things are "just so," this is it. So don't rush off to make copies of your resume until you complete the three editing steps outlined in this chapter.

## Step one: macro changes

Before you begin combing through your resume for typos and other micro changes, first reread your draft for a sense of the macro, the big picture. Have you painted a portrait of an accomplished, qualified job candidate who will meet the employer's needs? Don't forget: Your resume is a marketing tool—not a job description or autobiography. Focus on communicating the advantages you have to offer the employer.

Here are some of the macro questions to consider as you shape your resume into a final draft.

**1. Format.** Is your resume organized in a way that flatters you and clarifies your qualifications and strengths? Whether you use a chronological, functional or hybrid format, make sure that the flow of information won't raise questions or cause confusion.

**2. Length.** Is your resume longer than two pages? Are the pages suffocating with words and paragraphs, with little or no margins or line spaces for breathing room? Get out your pencil and start slashing. No matter how lengthy and illustrious your experience, find a way to tell your story more succinctly.

**3. Results.** Did you pepper your resume with results-oriented accomplishments? Will these achievements spell B-E-N-E-F-I-T-S to employers? If your resume reads like a job description, you've got work to do. Go back and include specific accomplishments that prove you made significant contributions to previous employers.

**4. Elements.** If you've included a job objective, is it targeted? Clear? Will it enhance your likelihood of getting an interview, or could it possibly eliminate you from consideration? If you've included a summary of qualifications, did you highlight the skills or experience most relevant to the job you're seeking? If you've chosen to list outside interests, memberships or awards and honors, does this information enhance your total package, or is it merely filling up space? If so, rewrite! Take out those nonselling points and replace them with more important, job-related accomplishments.

This big-picture review of your resume may lead you to extensive reorganization and rewriting. It may also drive you cross-eyed; after spending hour upon hour looking at the same material, it's hard to remain objective and clearheaded. This is a good time to ask for input from other people.

Show your resume to a few friends, family members or trusted co-workers, preferably those who are familiar with your skills and experience. These folks may help identify organization and content problems. They may also remind you of accomplishments or skills you have overlooked.

Yes, you may have the urge to strangle your "editors" when they suggest that you completely rewrite a portion of your resume. But investing the extra time to hammer out a stronger sales tool just may be the difference that lands you that dream job.

## Step two: a checklist for details

When you're satisfied that your resume is sound in structure and design, it's time to zoom in for a close-up look at the smaller—but still very significant—details. The following checklist will guide you through this micro editing phase.

### Name header

❑    Is your name header prominently placed at the top of the page?

❑    Did you use the most professional-sounding form of your name?

❑    Is your address correct? If you're about to move, did you put your current and soon-to-be address on your resume, and identify the dates you can be found at each?

❑    Did you list a phone number at which you can be reached easily, or at which a message can be left—a message that will be returned quickly? Did you include the area code? Make sure you haven't transposed any of the numbers.

## Job objective

❑ Is your job objective focused and precise, stating exactly the position you want?

❑ Does your objective mesh with the rest of your resume? Does your experience relate to your objective?

❑ Is your objective stated in 12 words or less?

❑ Are you sure you wouldn't be interested in any other positions? Are you confident that your job objective won't eliminate you from consideration from a position you might enjoy? If not, drop the objective.

## Skills summary

❑ Is your summary targeted to the job you're seeking? Does it highlight the qualifications and experience that are most important to your prospective employer?

❑ Is your summary short and concise (two or three brief sentences or four or five bulleted points)?

❑ Does your most relevant qualification come first in the summary?

## Experience profile

*Chronological Format*

❑ Did you include the correct starting and ending dates (month and year) for each work experience?

❑ Did you use your correct job title? If you "revised" it, did you choose a title that will not mislead or be considered deceitful?

❑ Did you include the correct name of your various employers, plus their company locations (if locations are not apparent from the company name)?

❑ Did you limit the job description section of each job listing to short sentences?

❑ Are any paragraphs longer than five lines?

*Functional and Hybrid Formats*

❑ Are the skill categories you chose the most relevant to the job you want?

❑ Did you use business-oriented labels for your skill category headings? For example, did you use "Childcare Experience" rather than "Baby-sitting Experience?" Use terminology applied in the business world, even if the meaning is the same.

❑ Did you include a brief chronological listing of your work experience (volunteer and paid) at the end of your resume?

*All Formats*

❑ Did you use strong action words to describe your contributions or achievements? Review the list of words on page 111 if you need to "energize" some of your verbs.

❑ Did you eliminate "I" from your language, as well as "the," "an" and other articles? Remember, use short, concise phrases to communicate your message.

❑ Did you use acronyms, initials or unfamiliar terms that might not be understood by the prospective employer? Eliminate words that may confuse. Spell out the name or phrase the first time, then put the acronym or initials in parentheses: "Broadway Commercial and Industrial Fittings (BCIF)."

❑ Did you repeat words, particularly your action words, over and over? Find a way to avoid repetition.

❑ Did you include, as much as possible, the specific benefits your accomplishments brought to your previous employers? For example, did you state the amount of money or time saved?

❑ When you listed an award or honor, did you explain why you were recognized? Did you use the correct name of the award? Did you put down the right date of the award?

## Education

❑ Did you verify the dates you earned your degree or attended school?

❑ Did you verify the type of degree earned, the school or institution attended and the location of the school?

❑ Did you double-check data related to certifications, licenses and other pertinent training?

## Other

❑ If you included memberships, did you double-check to make sure they're current affiliations and that you used the correct name of the organization?

❑ Did you include personal references? Pictures? Salary information? The heading "resume"? Testimonials? Reasons for leaving past positions? Get rid of them!

## Looks

(If you're having someone typeset your resume, make a list of formatting or layout instructions based on Chapter 11 and this listing.)

❑ Did you leave a one-inch margin at the top of your resume, and no less than a half-inch margin on all other borders?

❑ Did you use a readable type size: Go no smaller than 10-point type?

❑ Did you use a serif type face? (See page 127 for the definition.)

❑ Did you set the right margin ragged, rather than justified?

❑ Did you use boldface type wisely? When you scan your resume, what words jump out at you? Are these the words you want employers to notice first? If not, rethink your use of boldface type.

❑ Did you use underlining and all-caps sparingly—if at all—and only in section heads and in the name header?

❑ Did you break up blocks of information and sections with line spacing? Single-space within paragraphs and double-space between paragraphs and sections.

❑ Did you use bullets or asterisks to emphasize specific points within listings?

❑ If your resume is longer than one page, did you add the word *continued* at the bottom of page one, and add your name and *page 2* at the top of the second page?

❑ Are you consistent? Did you use the same line spacing, headline treatment, listing treatment, etc., throughout your resume? Did you put periods at the end of some accomplishment statements and leave them off others? Did you list one college degree in one format and use another for a second degree? Decide which styles you want to use, and check to be sure you have applied them religiously throughout all parts of the resume.

Chances are, you found plenty to change, correct, refine and condense on the first pass of your micro edit. After you've made those changes, you should read your resume again, with the same scrutiny as the first time.

But before you begin that second editing pass, take a break. Walk away from your resume. Read a magazine, take a nap, shop for a new interview suit, save a rain forest. Just give yourself a mental and physical rest—if possible, for a good 24 hours.

When you pick up your resume again, you'll be able to edit with a fresh eye and possibly catch a few more mistakes. Repeat this cycle until you're positive that you've got your final draft in your hands. Then, you're ready for step three.

# Step three: final proofread

Let us take this moment to remind you of something we know you've heard before. If the resume you submit to a prospective employer isn't completely error-free, you might as well kiss the job good-bye. So even though you are probably sick and tired of this whole resume business by now, it's essential that you take the time and effort to proofread your resume several times.

You've come so far. You've sculpted a masterful resume, packed it with sales points that will convince the employer that no one else can do the job as well as you. So why blow it because you mentioned *re-sluts* instead of *results*, because you used *there* instead of *their*, because you stated that you graduated in *1898* instead of *1989*?

Proofread thoroughly to make sure there are no remaining typos. Double-check all dates, phone numbers and names. Look for errors in spelling, punctuation and grammar.

Because you are now so familiar with your resume, your eye may have difficulty detecting problems. The following tips will help make your proofreading a success.

1. **Spell-check your resume.** If you're working on a computer, you may have access to a spell-check program, which will pick up misspelled words. Don't count on it, however, to help with *misused* words—*their* and *there,* for example—or misspelled proper names.

2. **Read your resume aloud.** Sounding out each word, syllable by syllable, helps in two ways. It makes identification of typos and misspelled words easier. And it makes awkward sentence structure and repetition of words jump out.

3. **Read backwards.** This is a great trick for catching misspellings and typos. Reading each word—from the end of your resume to the beginning—means you'll be focusing on the individual words rather than the meaning of phrases or sentences.

4. **Ask someone else to proofread, too.** Especially if you don't consider yourself particularly adept at proofreading, this is essential. In fact, ask as many people as you can to give your resume one last check.

After you've proofed your resume, make any corrections—and proofread again. Do this as many times as necessary, until you're willing to stake your next job on the fact that your resume is...perfect.

---

Chapter 13

# The Final Product:
# Printing Your Resume

Transforming your carefully constructed marketing tool into a tangible product—the actual resume that you will present to potential employers—takes as much thought and attention as any other step in the process of creating this document.

But how complicated could it be? All you have to do is print it, right? Basically, yes. But, as is the case with everything else in the job-search process, there are more effective ways to do this—and less effective ways.

Let the same principles that you followed to design your resume in Chapter 11 guide you as you prepare to print your resume. Let's review:

- Easy to read.
- Neat.
- Lots of white space.
- Clean.

You created an attractive resume look by making smart choices about margins, type and layout. Now you can enhance that look by making smart choices about printing your resume.

## First choice: Create and print on computer

Is there a "best" method for producing your resume? We think so. We recommend that you use a personal computer to create your resume, and a high-quality computer printer to reproduce it. This option gives you these advantages:

1. **You can make changes instantly.** You won't have to retype the entire resume because of one correction, as you would if you were working on a standard typewriter. You can play with different elements—changing headings, adjusting margins and rearranging information—until you get the exact look you want.

2. **It's simple to update your resume** or modify it to respond to specific job opportunities. You can create and store a "template," or standard version, of your resume, and then easily customize it as the need arises.

Ideally, your computer system should be equipped with a word-processing program and have the capability to print an appropriate serif typeface, such as Times Roman. You'll also need a laser printer or high-quality inkjet printer. Although you can use dot-matrix or so-called "letter-quality" printers to generate *working* copies of your resume—copies used in your writing and editing stages—these lower-end machines aren't acceptable for producing final copies you send to employers or networking contacts. They tend to produce type that is faded and difficult to read.

If you don't have a personal computer, beg access (and some operating assistance, if you're not very computer-literate) from a friend who has one. If the system you use doesn't have a laser or inkjet printer, you can store your resume on a computer disk, then ask a friend who does have the right equipment to print the resume from your disk. Most commercial copy centers and printers offer this document-printing service as well.

## Other means of reproducing your resume

If you're not fortunate enough to have access to a personal computer system, you have a few different options.

### Creating originals

To create master copies of your resume, you can:

**1. Use an office-quality typewriter.** If possible, use a newer-model machine that has memory capabilities. Don't use a manual typewriter or an older electric model. These machines often distribute ink unevenly, creating a splotchy, faded effect. If you have trouble finding a good typewriter, contact your public library. They may have a machine you can use or know where you can find one.

**2. Hire a professional word processor.** If you are truly a klutz at the keyboard or simply don't have the time or means to produce your own resume masters, there are plenty of people who will be happy to do the job. For reasons mentioned in the first part of this chapter, look for a professional who can give you a copy of your resume on computer disk as well as a hard (paper) copy. Be sure to agree on a price up front, and provide a list of exact design specifications. And proofread the finished product closely! You, not the word processor, are responsible for any errors.

**3. Have your resume typeset.** Commercial copy centers and printers can professionally typeset your resume from a handwritten or typed document. This option, although it will produce a fine resume, is expensive. And you won't be able to make changes easily and inexpensively, as you will if your resume is computer-generated. Because few people will notice a huge difference between a typeset document and one produced on a laser printer, you're better off to have your resume created by a professional word processor and then output on a laser printer.

## Making copies

To print copies of your original, your best option is to head for a commercial copy shop, also known as a "quick printer" or "offset printer." These printers generally offer a wide range of paper stocks and can print your copies while you wait or within a few hours. You may be offered a choice of ink colors; stick with black. Not only is it the least expensive, it's the most readable and most professional.

You may be contemplating printing copies of your resume on that copy machine in your office or at the library or drugstore. Don't! These machines typically are not well-maintained. You may end up with a resume that has smudges, streaks or inconsistent ink coverage.

## Printing don'ts

In addition to the rules we already mentioned regarding typewriters and low-end computer printers, your resume should absolutely, positively, never be:

- Handwritten.
- Copied on a Ditto machine.
- Duplicated by carbon paper.
- Mimeographed.

## Paper stock: the finishing touch

When selecting the paper stock for your resume, keep readability in the forefront of your thoughts. (Remember, easy to read, lots of white space, neat and clean.) In addition, your resume should look professional and conservative. The best way to convey these characteristics?

**1. Select white, off-white, ivory or buff-colored paper.** These colors not only ensure easier readability, they're the least likely to inflame personal bias. (Don't run the risk of sending your resume straight to the reject pile because the hirer hates pink...or gray...or blue.) If you are having your resume copied by an offset printer, be sure your master is printed on the brightest, whitest paper you can find. This will ensure the best reproduction.

**2. Choose a good-quality, medium-weight paper.** Use 24-pound weight paper, which is a little heavier than standard copy paper. Most printers carry this paper stock, and you can usually find it at large office-supply stores also. You should have no trouble finding a paper stock that feels expensive—but isn't.

**3. Select a paper stock with a conservative finish.** A textured paper is okay as long as the texture is simple and does not hinder readability.

**4. Make sure matching stationery and envelopes are available.** You need matching stationery for your cover letters—and matching envelopes to complete the professional look of your resume package. (Putting together your cover letters and mailing out your resumes is coming up next!)

## Don't touch it once it's done!

It's finished...your resume, your baby. Don't make a single mark on it! Don't pencil in a note, write in an updated phone number or try to cover up a spelling error with correction fluid. If you must change something on your resume, go back to the computer, the typewriter, the printer, whatever. The resume you send out must be perfect, flawless, pristine, virgin, untouched.

Yes, of course employers will spill coffee, fold, mutilate and scribble notes all over your masterpiece. But *you* can't. We never said life was fair.

# Part III:

# The Job Hunt

Chapter 14

# Networking and Other Job-Search Strategies

You've done it. You've whittled and honed and polished your resume into a masterful sales piece. You are now well-armed with confidence and have a clear vision of where you've been and where you want to go. But your job-search journey has just begun.

It doesn't do you any good to have the right tools if you don't use them. So now, you must get out there and beat the bushes for job leads.

In Chapter 2, we addressed some traditional—and frequently ineffective—job-search strategies: responding to classified ads, approaching personnel offices and mass-mailing your resume to hundreds of employers. In this chapter, we'll examine some new and better ways to track down job opportunities. We'll also look at how you can update those traditional job-hunting tactics to make them more productive.

## Networking: looking for jobs in all the right places

If you're typical of many women, the term *networking* may bring a negative image to mind. Perhaps you picture a cocktail-party atmosphere: lots of schmoozing, air-kissing phonies with coat-hanger smiles "working" the room, sharing intimate conversation with 50 or more of their closest friends. Maybe you envision a dark-paneled, over-stuffed, members-only men's club, where good old boys meet for drinks and trade business favors. Or you might even imagine a chain letter, in which you're blackmailed with threats of bad karma into doing something you don't want to do for people you don't even know.

Maybe it's the "nice girl" syndrome again. But women often consider networking to be exploitive or manipulative. It may seem that you are "using" someone to further your own means.

But think about it. You wouldn't hesitate to ask a friend for the name of a good dentist or reputable lawyer. If you've recently hired a building contractor, scheduled an appointment with a new hairdresser, or signed your kids up for a summer camp, chances are you asked for recommendations from friends, family, acquaintances and even friends of friends of friends. You probably network all the time and don't even realize it.

The problem, perhaps, is how you define networking. Our definition doesn't include sucking up to people you can't stand just to get an introduction to some CEO. It doesn't mean pestering strangers on the bus or shoving your business card down the throat of everyone you meet. What it does mean is simply this: You let personal and professional acquaintances know that you are looking for a job. And you ask them to alert you if they hear of any suitable openings and to give you the names of contacts who may need someone with your skills.

Networking is not a dirty word. It has to do with team playing. Sharing important information. Helping each other reach our goals. This time, you're the one asking for help; next time, you'll lend a hand. So shake off any feelings of guilt, any images of exploitation, and get out there and network!

## Word-of-mouth: your best source of job leads

Why is networking such an effective job-search strategy? Why do we recommend it more than any other approach? Ask any salesperson. Word-of-mouth referrals are the best form of advertising. That's what you get when you network—a referral. And, in a sense, an endorsement from someone your potential employer knows and respects. The employer thinks, "Well, so-and-so thinks enough of this person to introduce her to me, so she must be worth talking to." You gain instant credibility—and often, a key to doors that otherwise might be tightly locked against job-seekers.

In addition, when you're networking, you've got a sales force behind you. There's a whole group of people out there looking for opportunities for you, recommending you to people they know. You're not alone.

Remember when we talked about how the majority of jobs are never advertised, but instead get filled by the "somebody-knows-somebody" system? You'll be surprised at how many of these "hidden" jobs you'll uncover through networking. But—and this is very important—building an effective job network requires some effort and sensitivity on your part. Although successful networking is mostly a matter of old-fashioned common sense, here are a few tips to help you get started.

## 1. Start with people you know.

Make a list of everyone you might possibly ask for job leads—friends, family, college pals, professional or social contacts, former teachers, past employers. Don't overlook anyone! You may think that your grandmother, who hasn't worked since 1949, is an unlikely source of information. But her *mah jongg* buddy's son may be a director in a corporation that has a place for you.

## 2. Make an entry in your career file.

Include the name, address and home phone number of each of these initial contacts. If applicable, also add the contact's job title and business address and phone.

## 3. When approaching contacts, ask:

*"Do you know anyone who may be looking for someone with my qualifications?"*

*"Do you know anyone who might know anyone looking for someone with my qualifications?"*

You may not get many "yes" responses to the first question. Perhaps none of your initial contacts knows of an employer who might need your talents. But many of them are likely to answer positively to the second question and be able to give you at least a few leads—names of people who might know someone with employment opportunities. Write the names of these secondary contacts at the bottom of the initial contact's Career Card.

After talking with all of your initial contacts, you should have a decent list of secondary contacts. Great! Fill out a Career Card for each of these new people. Note on the card who gave you the contact name. You can also jot down any miscellaneous background information that your initial contact was able to provide about the individual.

## 4. Investigate every lead.

Now, get on the phone and follow up on these leads. (You can also approach contacts by mail, but a phone call is better. It's quicker and allows you to get an immediate response.) Always begin the conversation by mentioning the name of the person who suggested you call. Have your Career Cards in front of you, so this information will be available. Establishing that you have a mutual acquaintance should lower the contact's professional guard and lead to a friendlier, warmer response to your inquiry. What do you say to these friends of friends?

Something like this: "I'm searching for new career opportunities, and Bob thought you might have some ideas on where to look."

## 5. Get information interviews.

When you are referred to a contact at a company that you may be interested in joining, ask that contact if it would be possible to arrange an information interview—not a job interview. Explain to the contact that you are interested in finding out more about his or her company and department. Most people will be agreeable to this.

## 6. Do your research.

Before the information interview, find out everything you can about the company, its products or services, its competition and its problems. You should be able to ask intelligent questions during your interview.

Where do you find this data? Head to the library. Read any articles that have been written about the company or its officers and review reports in business-reference guides, such as *Standard & Poor's Register of Corporations, Directors and Executives*. (The appendix at the back of this book contains a list of possible resources.) You also can call the company directly. Ask for an annual report, a corporate brochure—what the heck, see if you can get your hands on an employee manual.

## 7. Conduct the interview.

Remember, this is not a job interview! You're not ready to ask for a job yet. In this scenario, you're the interviewer—not the interviewee. (Job interview strategies are discussed in Chapter 16.)

In the information interview, your objective is to find out whether this employer will be a good match for you, to discover what problems you may be able to solve, and to learn whether there are any upcoming openings in your area at the company. You might want to ask about management philosophies, corporate structure or future growth plans. Of course, you should focus some of your questions specifically on the department you want to join. Draw out your contact, too, asking what he or she enjoys most about working for the company.

Don't kid yourself, though. You know darn well that the end result you are seeking is a job. (And quite frankly, the contact will assume the same.) Prepare for an information interview as if it were a job interview. Dress professionally. Conduct yourself professionally. And without forcing the conversation, try to mention an accomplishment that may

be relevant to the topic of discussion. But don't just talk about yo
self—remember, you're supposed to be gathering information.

## 8. What if you hit the jackpot?

If, oh happy day, you actually fall upon a real-live job possibility
during an information interview, keep your cool. Suppose, for example,
that your brother-in-law's fraternity pal, who happens to be the
claims adjuster at a large insurance company, has agreed to meet you
for an information interview over lunch. In the middle of the main
course, he mentions an upcoming opening at his firm, and says that
you definitely should apply. Don't choke on your linguini or fall to your
knees in thanks.

Express your interest and ask whom you should approach regarding the job opening. If your contact just happens to be the hiring
manager (my, you have been living right!), ask how you can throw
your hat in the ring. Then return the focus to the purpose of your
meeting: to get information. Of course, if the hiring manager wants to
pursue your interest right then and there, go for it. *Carpe diem*, as
they say.

## 9. Leave your resume.

At the end—not the beginning—of your meeting, give your resume to the contact. Ask that it be passed along to anyone who might
be interested in your skills (better yet, bring extra copies of your resume to give to the contact). And conclude the interview by asking
whether the contact knows of any other leads you should investigate.

## 10. Thank everyone!

After any interaction, whether it's an in-person interview or phone
call, send off a brief thank-you note. Thank the contact for sharing
information about the company and/or employment opportunities, say
that you will stay in touch and ask to be advised if any new opportunities arise.

Don't forget to thank the person who referred you to the contact as
well. While most people are happy to help out a friend, your acknowl-
edgment will be appreciated—and remembered.

## 11. Keep in touch.

Touch base with your networking contacts regularly. You don't want
to be a nudge, but a short phone call from time to time is helpful. If you
feel uncomfortable about this, you should be able to find an excuse to

call—alert the contact to an upcoming trade association meeting, pass along some news that may be useful, or express your thanks for a lead or piece of advice that proved particularly helpful. These follow-up calls will keep you in the forefront of your contacts' minds and possibly remind them of additional leads.

### 12. Follow up leads immediately.

Whenever a contact alerts you to a specific job opening, follow up on it immediately. When applying, introduce yourself by saying that your contact suggested that you pursue the position. Don't let hot leads get cold—the sooner you respond, the better your chances of slipping in ahead of the competition!

### 13. Respect your contacts.

The number-one rule of successful networking is treating all of your contacts with respect. Don't abuse connections by harassing or pestering busy people. Be sensitive of everyone's time. When speaking on the phone, be brief and to the point. When meeting with a contact, show up on time, and don't exceed the agreed-upon time allotment. Don't manipulate situations, implying that you have a closer relationship with a mutual connection than you really have or pressuring individuals for opportunities because of some obligation to a friend. If you burn your contacts, your sources for job-search information will dry up quickly.

## Beyond networking: other job-search strategies

With luck—not to mention a lot of hard work on your part—your network contacts will keep your schedule buzzing with both information interviews and job interviews. But to build a broader base of job leads, you may want to explore other employment avenues as well. Let's look at three alternate routes: cold-contact campaigns, classified ads and employment services.

## Cold-contact marketing

Sending out scores of resumes to potential employers, with no prior introduction from a networking contact, *can* turn up good job leads. But as we told you in Chapter 2, this mass-mailing strategy (also known as "broadcast mailing") must be handled correctly, or it will be a flop.

Whether you make hundreds of these "cold-contact" inquiries—or just a few—this approach only works if you follow these three rules:

1. **Target your market carefully.** Targeting, you'll recall, means sending your resume only to those employers who are good prospects for your product. Don't waste your time or money selling to people who have no reason to buy.

2. **Contact a specific person.** It's imperative that you get your resume to the person responsible for hiring decisions—not to "whomever it may concern."

3. **Personalize your inquiry.** You must tailor your cover letters and your phone calls to each individual company. You must let the company know that you understand its particular needs— and show how you can solve those needs. You can't do that with a generic, one-size-fits-all approach.

There's actually one more rule to the cold-contact approach. Just as you did when approaching your networking contacts, you should request an information interview before you send off your resume. Why? Because this "warms up" cold contacts, making them far more receptive to looking at your resume.

## Building your target list

How do you find out what companies are most likely to need your services? Research. Again, your public library should have many resources that will help you find likely targets for your marketing campaign.

You should be able to unearth the names and addresses of companies involved in particular industries, as well as descriptions of company products. Often, you can find out a company's annual sales figures, contact names, number of employees and even employment qualifications. Tell the librarian what you're doing, and ask which resources will offer the best data. Also, try to get your hands on company brochures and other sales literature, as when preparing for your information interviews.

When evaluating your research, you may need to read between the lines to determine who is, and who isn't, a good prospect. What are some clues to look for? For starters, is the company growing? It may be more likely to be hiring. Does the company specialize in some area in which you have impressive expertise? It's a good bet they'll want to meet you. If the company is in bankruptcy, on the other hand, or just laid off 500 workers, you should cross it off your list!

How large should your target list be? That's entirely up to you. Obviously, the more companies you contact, the more likely you are to succeed.

## What's in a name?

In this case, everything! You must find a specific contact at each company. Otherwise, your resume is going to wind up in the wrong file, lost forever in corporate limbo or pitched in the trash can.

You need to figure out who is the most appropriate hiring manger for you to contact. If you weren't able to determine this in your previous research, you can:

**1. Check with your networking contacts.** Do they know anyone who works at this company? Call that person and ask for the name of the hiring manager.

**2. Call the company directly.** If you've discovered that Bader Bingo, Inc., has a growing customer service department, and you're interested in working there, call the company and ask for the name of the director of the department. Usually, a receptionist or secretary will happily give this information out. If he or she seems hesitant to help you, simply say that you have some information that may be of value to the company, and you want to make sure it gets to the right person. Remember to verify the spelling of the contact's name during your call.

## Making contact

If you've done your research properly, you should now have a good, targeted list of companies and hiring managers. Now, you have two choices: contact those hiring managers by phone or by mail. Either way, your goal is the same as when approaching networking contacts: an information interview.

**1. Phone prospecting.** Contacting your prospects by phone is undoubtedly the best way to go. Use the same approach as you would if you were calling one of your networking leads. Introduce yourself, say that you are interested in finding out more about the contact's company and department, and ask if it would be possible to arrange an information interview. The difference, of course, is that you don't have a name of a mutual acquaintance to use as a door-opener. But if you present your request so the person doesn't feel pressured or obligated, you're likely to get a meeting.

**2. Mail contacts.** If it's impossible for you to contact your prospects by phone, you can make your request by mail. (For an idea of how to structure your request, see the sample letter in the next chapter.) End your inquiry letter by saying that you will call in one week to see whether the contact is agreeable to meeting with you. Don't include your resume in any correspondence yet. Save it for your information interview, as before. Be sure to call on the day you mentioned in the letter. Don't wait any longer—you want to call while your name and letter are fresh in the prospect's mind.

Whether you prospect by phone or mail, conduct your information interview—and follow-up campaign—in the same manner as you would with a networking contact.

## If a meeting isn't possible...

If you're contacting employers in another state, a face-to-face information interview may not be possible. In that case, try to conduct the interview over the phone. Then follow up by mailing your resume and thank-you letter.

What if the contact won't agree to an informational interview? Ask for the names of other people in the company you might contact, then send the first individual a thank-you note, enclosing a copy of your resume for good measure.

## Turn every lead into a contact

After you've "warmed up" cold contacts, treat them as you would your networking contacts. Stay in touch with letters and phone calls to firm up the relationship. And by all means add this contact's name to your Career Card file—it just may lead you to a job down the road.

# Classified ads

It may be true that only a small percentage of available jobs are advertised in the classified ads. But positions are filled this way, so there's no need to forgo this job-search route altogether. Just take steps to increase your chances of landing the job.

First, expand your definition of "want ads." Search the classified sections of trade and association journals as well as newspapers. And don't overlook the weekday newspaper editions—most people wait until Sunday to review the classifieds, meaning there may be more competition for those jobs.

When responding to an ad, don't just contact the personnel department. In addition, try to find out the name of the hiring manager, and approach that person directly as well. Use the same techniques described in the cold-contact section to track down "the name." Once you get this name, you can send the hiring manager a cover letter and resume. Your hope is that the contact will personally open your letter and be so impressed with your qualifications that he or she demands that HR schedule you for an interview immediately.

What's more likely to happen is this: The hiring manager will recognize your correspondence as a response to the ad, perhaps take a minute to review it, then pass it on to HR and ask them to follow up. This communication to HR may not be as enthusiastic as you'd hoped, but you've still increased your chances of getting an interview. Why? Simply because your name was brought to HR's attention by the hiring manager.

## The back-door approach

Here's another tactic recommended by some job-search experts: To avoid the risk of getting waylaid by HR, use the "back-door" approach. Call the hiring manager and request an information interview. Whatever you do, however, don't refer to this meeting as an "interview." Your goal is to meet the decision-maker without having to go through HR—but because of company policies or politics, the individual may not be willing to meet with you if it's apparent that you actually want to apply for the job opening.

The idea, of course, is to get yourself "in the right place at the right time"—subtly. What? They just happen to have an opening for someone like you? What a coincidence! *Voilà*—you've just put yourself ahead of the pack, because you know the hiring manager.

Is this an ethical approach, you ask? Well, admittedly, it's a bit shy of completely honest. To avoid compromising your integrity—and coming off like a scam artist—don't try to turn the information interview into a job interview. As we recommended before, should the topic of the job opening come up during the information interview, say that you'd be interested in the position, and for an opportunity to discuss it. Then continue on with your information-gathering process.

## Blind ads: in-the-dark responses

How do you respond to so-called "blind ads"—ads in which the hiring company is not identified? How is it possible to track down the name of the decision-maker when you're directed to send your resume to a newspaper box number? It isn't.

Most job-search experts advise you not to waste your time responding to such ads. Often, employers are merely using them to gather information on salary expectations or to gauge the quality of the candidate pool. If it is a legitimate ad, you run the risk of responding to your own company—or someone who is connected with your boss.

If you're convinced there's nothing to lose, it won't hurt to respond to an ad that seems to describe your ideal job. But don't hold your breath.

# Headhunters and other employment services

Headhunters, executive search firms, executive recruiters, employment consultants, placement agencies. There are a number of names for businesses that assist others in finding jobs—or help businesses find qualified employees. Not all of them work the same way.

### Executive search firms

Also known as headhunters, these firms are really working for the employer. Companies pay them to find qualified candidates for certain positions, usually at the executive or managerial level. If you register with this kind of firm, you'll be added to its data banks of available personnel, and you may very well be called if the firm feels you are a top candidate for a particular job. Try to hook up with a firm that specializes in recruiting people in your field. But understand that the search firm's main responsibility is to meet the employer's needs—not to look for suitable jobs for you.

### Employment agencies

Placement, or employment, agencies serve more as a matchmaking service—taking both employers and employees as clients. These companies are more likely to work actively on your behalf. However, use caution. While as a rule, it's the employer who pays for the agency's services, sometimes the job candidate is required to pay a fee. If you choose to work with an employment agency, make sure you find out exactly what you're getting into. Before you sign any contract or agreement, read it carefully and understand the terms.

### Employment consultants

If you find the right kind of consulting firm, you may find its services helpful in expanding your job search. But beware of offers to supply you with lists of "hidden" job opportunities for a fee. The money you pay may not be worth the assistance you receive. You probably can find the same opportunities—or even better ones—on your own.

### Temporary agencies

Temporary employment agencies, such as Manpower and Kelly Services, can be a great place to find temporary work. Usually, the jobs these agencies fill are clerical in nature, but more and more, you can also find temporary assignments in more specialized areas, such as accounting, management consulting and the like. If your budget is running low, a temporary assignment can be just the ticket to fill the gaps. Another benefit: It's a great way to get to know employers and job contacts! Many temporary assignments lead to full-time opportunities, too.

## Stay in charge

Perhaps the biggest drawback to working with any employment service is that you may be tempted to become a passive, uninvolved job seeker. If you rely on others to do the work for you, you may find that nothing is happening. Many agencies instruct you to let them follow up on any job leads you uncover—and they may not follow up as well or as promptly as you might yourself. So even if you work with an agency or other service, you must continue to actively search out your own opportunities.

## Chapter 15

# Selling by Mail: Cover Letters, Follow-up Calls and More

In many cases, you'll approach your contacts by phone or in person. But other times, you'll need to market yourself by mail. Whether you're writing to request an information interview or to apply for a specific job opening, this correspondence needs to be handled with the same sales smarts that you've applied to the rest of your job search.

In this chapter, you'll learn how to write cover letters and requests for information interviews in a way that gets the response you want. You'll also learn what you can do to improve your odds of landing an interview once your letter's in the mail.

## Request for information interviews

Let's look first at how to handle what will probably be your initial piece of job-search correspondence: the request for an information interview.

In this letter, you need to introduce yourself, explain why you're writing and request the interview. If you are writing at the suggestion of a networking contact, you should open the letter by mentioning that person's name.

Use a standard business-correspondence layout (consult a business-letter reference book if you're unfamiliar with your options). But keep the tone friendly and relaxed—as if you were writing to the cousin of a good friend, perhaps. Keep the letter to one page, and always close by stating that you will call to request a meeting time.

Don't try to "sell" yourself in this letter. Remember that your goal is to establish a relationship and gather information. It's fine to include a little bit of background about yourself, but keep it brief. Don't forget to include your name, address and phone number, so that the contact can reach you if needed.

An example of an effective introductory letter is on the next page. Without being gimmicky, Rebecca grabs Christine's attention by referring to Bert, a mutual contact, right off the bat. She quickly explains her purpose for writing and her connection with Bert, while simultaneously establishing her interest and experience in interior decorating.

In a nonthreatening, polite manner, Rebecca asks for the information interview. She makes it clear that she wants nothing more from Christine at this point than a little advice. She also takes responsibility for setting up the meeting, and establishes a timeline for her follow-up phone call. The overall tone of the letter is casual, enthusiastic, and, yes, flattering to the reader.

---

Rebecca Spencer
54 Blaine Street
Augusta, GA 30901
404-555-3271

Christine Dyken                                         July 19, 1995
C. D. & Associates
24 Twelve Oaks Lane, Ste. 210
Augusta, GA 30901

Dear Ms. Dyken:

When I asked Bert Keilor for advice on getting started in interior decorating, he said, "there's no one who knows the business better than Christine Dyken." With that glowing recommendation in mind, I'm writing to see if you might be willing to share some of your professional insights with me.

For the last two years, I've been in the process of restoring and redecorating a 100-year-old home. (Bert handled the sunroom addition and did a beautiful job!) This experience reaffirmed my love for interior design, and I'm now pursuing it as a full-time career.

I'm excited about my new direction, yet I have dozens of questions about how to proceed. From what Bert says, you'd be a great source of information—and inspiration. Would it be possible for us to get together some time soon so I can pick your brain a bit?

I'll call you next week, and if you're agreeable, we can set a time to meet. If it's not possible for us to meet in person, perhaps we can chat for a few minutes over the phone.

Thank you so much for your time. I look forward to speaking with you soon.

Sincerely,

*Rebecca Spencer*

Rebecca Spencer

---

What if you were approaching a cold contact and had no name to "drop" in the introductory paragraph? You can use an introduction like this:

*Dear Ms. Pepple:*

*Based on what I've read and heard, Pepple Cuisine is one of the top catering firms in town. As someone who is interested in exploring catering as a possible career field, I'm hoping that you might be willing to offer a bit of information and advice.*

# The cover letter: a proper introduction for your resume

Job-search etiquette requires that your resume always receive a proper introduction. And when you can't give it an in-person introduction, handing it directly to a networking contact or interviewer, your resume should always be accompanied by its chaperone: the cover letter.

The cover letter explains why you are sending your resume. But there's more to it than that. If written correctly, it also helps to sell your skills and qualifications and to get you noticed by the hirer.

For some reason, cover letters seem to be a great source of mystery to most job-seekers. It is as though there were a secret formula that only enlightened professionals—namely the job-givers—are privy to. Job-hunters seem to fear the cover letter as much as medieval peasants feared eclipses. Perhaps you, too, are sure that your cover letter will blot out your chances of being chosen for an interview.

Although there is indeed a formula to use when writing a cover letter, there's about as much mystery to it as taking two aspirin for a headache. It's just a matter of keeping in mind the same marketing principle we've been stressing throughout this book: Keep the needs of the customer—in your case, the potential employer—in mind.

# 10 steps to more powerful cover letters

**1. Personalize the cover letter.** Never, never address the cover letter to "Dear Sir or Madam," or "To Whom it May Concern." Always address the letter to a specific person—presumably, this will be the hiring manager. For a reminder on how to track down contact names, review Chapter 14.

**2. Immediately clarify why you're writing.** In the very first sentence of your letter, state why you're writing. Make it short and sweet—business people don't have time to wade through a lot of verbose mumbo-jumbo. Here are two examples of intros that effectively communicate their purpose:

> *"Your ad in* The Times *for a director of summer camp programs caught my attention."*

> *"Julie Brooks suggested I contact you about your search for a computer programmer."*

**3. Let the reader know there's a benefit coming.** It's the old "what's in it for me" philosophy again. Not only does the introduction need to clarify why you're writing, it must do it in a way that alerts the reader that there's a possible benefit for the company involved.

The wrong approach:

> *"I have always wanted to work as a restaurant hostess at an establishment like yours."*

Does the employer really care what the job hunter wants? No. The employer is interested in finding a competent hostess. Although the writer is quite complimentary of the reader's restaurant, it's more prudent to put the reader's interests first.

The right approach:

> *"Your ad in Sunday's* Tribune *announced your need for an efficient, personable hostess. I'm writing because I can offer you those exact qualifications, plus several years of experience in the restaurant business."*

If you have some trouble with this concept, write whatever introduction comes naturally to you. Then, see if you can structure the paragraph or sentence so that the word "you" or "your" comes first.

**4. Set the tone in the first line.** First impressions count the most. And while reading the first sentence of your letter, the hirer is already beginning to develop a picture, a feeling about you. Make sure it's a good one. You want to come across to the reader as someone who is both professional and pleasant—a good person to work with.

The wrong approach:

*"Upon reviewing your advertisement for an insurance underwriter, I hereby wish to express my interest in such a position with your esteemed company."*

*"Your prayers are answered! I'm the person you've been waiting for to send your sales figures skyrocketing."*

*"Your department store is the most high-class operation I've ever seen and I'd give anything to be a part of your enterprise."*

Whew! Do these people sound like anyone you'd like to work with? Avoid sounding too stilted. Or too cocky. Or too desperate.

*The right approach:* Your tone should be friendly, direct and professional. Try this:

*"Your ad for an experienced underwriter prompted me to contact you."*

**5. Highlight qualifications related to the position you want.** You identify why you're writing in the introduction paragraph. In the next few paragraphs, summarize your qualifications for the position you're seeking.

The key here is to let the reader know that you offer a good solution to the company's needs. You need to stress the most important benefits that you can bring to the company. Make sure the points you include here are specific and targeted toward this particular employer and position.

Here are a few suggestions:

- Mention impressive accomplishments that are related to the job or department you're targeting.
- Explain how you meet qualifications described in the company's job advertisement.
- Use the buzzwords and terminology of your industry. Don't overdo it. But make it clear that you speak the language.

Avoid vague references to your workstyle or potential—"hardworking, detail-oriented, loyal." You cut this no-sale verbiage from your resume—don't let it sneak back in to muddle up your cover letter.

**6. Don't tell the whole story.** Your objective in the cover letter is to intrigue the reader. Don't reiterate everything that's in your resume.

Just pull out the best of the best. And don't merely lift phrases verbatim from your resume; reword them so they sound fresh.

**7. Sidestep requests for salary information.** Many employers will tell you that you need to include salary history or requirements in your cover letter in order to be considered for a job. Although you shouldn't completely ignore this request, you shouldn't answer it specifically, either. For reasons you will learn in the next chapter, when we discuss salary issues, you should never name a salary figure until you are offered the job.

You can handle this situation in one of two ways. You can state an acceptable salary range, leaving a lot of leeway for negotiation—for example, "I would expect that an appropriate salary for a position such as this would be in the $30,000 to $40,000 range." Or you can simply explain that you will be happy to discuss salary requirements once you have a better understanding of the position. Again, we'll get into this issue more in Chapter 16.

**8. Close with a commitment to action.** *Your* action, that is. Don't expect the reader to take the responsibility to jump on the phone and schedule an interview with you. You take the lead by concluding your letter something like this:

> *"I will call you next week to see if we can arrange a time to discuss this position in person."*

One reminder: Even though you are taking the responsibility to call the employer, don't forget to include your full name, address and phone number in the return address on your letter! The employer just may want to contact you first.

**9. Keep it short.** Your cover letter should not exceed one page. Each paragraph should be short, no longer than four or five lines. Consider the rules you followed in designing your resume: Lots of white space. Short lines. Easy-to-read. Apply these same rules to your cover letter as well.

**10. Make sure it's error-free!** Proofread closely. Look for typos and misspelled names. Don't add any last-minute notes in pencil or try to insert a missed comma or period with your black pen. Produce your cover letter on the same printer that you printed your resume, and use the same serif typeface. Print your cover letter on the same paper stock, and send off both documents in a matching envelope.

# Cover letter samples

On the next two pages are two versions of the same cover letter, showing two different design and layout possibilities. For these examples, imagine that the writer is responding to the following job ad:

*Wanted: Professional receptionist for busy graphic design firm. Responsible for phone coverage, appointment scheduling and miscellaneous billing and paperwork. Computer skills a plus.*

Let's also assume that this job-seeker is following up on a "cold" lead—she has no networking introduction to the employer.

---

Jennifer Lin
530 Nassau Lane
Louisville, KY 40231
606-555-0870

Mr. Bruce Johnson                                         August 26, 1995
Johnson Dean Design, Inc.
3400 South Bend Ave.
Louisville, KY 40231

Dear Mr. Johnson:

Your ad in last Sunday's Louisville Courier-Journal explained that you need a professional receptionist who also has the ability to handle multiple office projects. I can bring just that kind of experience and ability to your firm.

For the past five years, I've been a receptionist and office assistant at a busy medical practice. In addition to handling the phones for three family practitioners, I also schedule appointments and handle paperwork and billing. Last year, I decreased time spent on billing by 25 percent by creating new invoicing and accounts payable systems.

As you can imagine, this job requires the ability to maintain a professional phone demeanor under pressure and to juggle many different priorities. It also provided the opportunity to use computerized accounting programs, another skill that should prove useful in your office.

The enclosed resume details other qualifications I can offer you. After you've had a chance to review it, I'd like to meet with you in person to discuss the position. I will call you next Monday to try to schedule a meeting.

In the meantime, thank you for your consideration.

Sincerely,

*Jennifer Lin*

Jennifer Lin

---

Jennifer immediately refers to the purpose of her letter—a response to the recent ad for a receptionist. She positions her opening in a way that focuses on the employer's needs rather than her own desire to find a job.

Then, Jennifer addresses her qualifications, citing examples of how they relate to the design firm's needs. She refers to the want ad, explains why she meets the criteria in the ad and mentions an accomplishment as proof of her abilities. Jennifer concludes her letter with an action statement. She assumes responsibility for setting up a meeting, rather than expecting Mr. Johnson to contact her.

Now, let's look at the body of the same letter, adapted slightly and presented in a different format.

---

Dear Mr. Johnson:

Your ad in last Sunday's Louisville Courier-Journal explained that you need a professional receptionist who also has the ability to handle multiple office projects.

As you can see from the enclosed resume, I can offer you the exact qualifications you're seeking:

Receptionist skills: For the past five years, I've been a receptionist at a busy medical practice.

Office administration skills: In addition to handling the phones for three family practitioners, I also schedule appointments and handle paperwork and billing. Last year, I decreased time spent on billing by 25 percent by creating new invoicing and accounts payable systems.

Computer skills: I'm familiar with computerized accounting programs, another skill that should prove useful in your office.

After you've had a chance to review my resume, I'd like to meet with you in person to discuss this position. I will call you next Monday to try to schedule a meeting.

In the meantime, thank you for your consideration.


Sincerely,

*Jennifer Lin*

Jennifer Lin

---

This layout makes it a little easier for the reader to spot Jennifer's important skills and qualifications—a plus when your resume lands on the desk of a busy person. However, the traditional format should be just as effective, as long as you keep your paragraphs short, punchy, benefits-oriented and to-the-point. Use whatever style seems to fit your situation best.

# Follow-up calls: dialing for interviews

After you send off your carefully constructed marketing letters, you can't sit back and wait for the phone to ring. You must keep your word and call that contact on the specified date.

Your goal is to set a firm appointment for an interview. If you're requesting an information interview, you should have no problem. When you get your contacts on the phone, just remind them of who you are and what you want. You'll find that most people will be glad to grant this sort of interview, if you've approached them in the right way.

Dialing for job interviews, however, is a bit tougher, as you know if you've ever tried to do this. It's doubly so if you've had no previous personal communication with the hirer, either through a networking contact or an information interview. The person on the other end of the line will most likely try to cut you off as soon as possible. They may be reluctant to agree to an interview right then and there—they may try to avoid making a decision.

So why not take the easy way out, and let the employer call you? Because there are two big payoffs to taking the pro-active approach. First, you'll be marked as a professional, someone who is well-versed in the art of business communication. Second, and perhaps most important, very few job seekers make the effort to do this sort of follow-up. Which means that you'll be even more impressive and noticeable to your prospective employer.

Remember, the competition for any job is steep. You can't afford to sit back and wait for your ship to come in—you've got to swim out after it. So, on to the swimming lesson! Here are a few effective strategies you can use when you call to ask for that job interview.

## Ask for 60 seconds of their time

When you get the contact on the phone, first ask whether your resume has been received. After the contact verifies that your resume indeed arrived, ask for 60 seconds to run through your qualifications and arrange a time for an interview.

Here's how you might approach a typical phone call:

You: *Mr. Brown, this is Susan Jones. I'm calling regarding the marketing assistant position at your firm. I forwarded my resume to you last week, and I want to be sure that you received it.*

Mr. Brown: *Yes, I did, and if you're selected for an interview, you'll be contacted.*

You: *I'd appreciate that. But if I could take 60 seconds of your time now, though, I'd like to briefly recap my qualifications for you. Then if you agree that I can solve your accounting needs, we can save time and go ahead and schedule a time to meet right now.*

At this point, most Mr. Browns will grant you that 60 seconds. The exception is the Mr. Brown who works as a screener in a personnel office and receives a zillion calls from hopeful candidates each day. This points up again the importance of getting your resume to the direct hiring manager.

When you do get the go-ahead to continue the conversation, it's vital that you make the most of your 60 seconds. Pick major accomplishments or skills that directly relate to the position in question. Specifically state how those skills could benefit the employer.

For example, suppose you know that Mr. Brown's company sells office machines to businesses across the country. You also know that they're looking for a marketing assistant to do the following: assist with daily correspondence; coordinate mass mailings to sales prospects; track sales; and maintain a computerized database of sales and clients. Your 60-second speech might go something like this:

*"I have two years experience as an administrative assistant in a business-to-business service firm. In my current position, I organize several large mailings each year; one markets our services to 500,000 businesses in the U.S. I've implemented several new procedures that saved my company on postage costs. I also reformatted our marketing database so that it is easier for sales reps to use. My manager attributed a dramatic increase in sales efficiency to that change."*

*"In addition, I have computer skills, word-processing experience and other qualifications that would benefit your company—but since I promised to only take 60 seconds of your time, I'll save those till we meet in person. If you're interested, why don't we set a time to get together now?"*

Notice that this speech addresses Mr. Brown's specific needs in terms of your specific accomplishments and their benefits.

Always wrap up by repeating your request to schedule an interview date. In marketing lingo, this is known as "asking for the sale." You can't get a "yes" answer unless you ask the question.

At the end of your 60 seconds, Mr. Brown will either: 1) agree to an interview; 2) say that he'll review your resume and call you if he wants to interview you further; 3) say "thanks, but no thanks;" or 4) ask questions. Of course, outcome #1 is your goal, but #4 is also ideal, because it gives you a chance to continue with your sales presentation.

Even if you hear response #2, however, Mr. Brown is likely to remember you when he sorts through that stack of resumes again. If you've conducted yourself politely and professionally, that's bound to make points in your favor.

What if Mr. Brown flat out refuses you as an interview candidate? Ask what specific qualifications you are lacking. Find out if there are other departments in his company that might benefit from someone with your qualifications. This information will help you evaluate your job search and your resume.

### Yes, we have no jobs

Unless you've sent your resume in response to a specific job opening, there's no way to know whether a potential employer is actively hiring. Your follow-up phone call may net you the standard line: "We're not hiring right now, but we'll keep your resume on file."

Don't hang up! Instead, use this as an opportunity to get an information interview (unless, of course, you've already gone that route with this particular contact). You might say something like:

> *"I understand that there are no positions available. But I'm very interested in your organization and would like to meet with you for a half-hour or so anyway. That way, we both can get a better idea of whether you could use a person like me on your team someday. Could we set a date to do that?"*

Again, it's important to close your request with a specific request for an interview date. Don't leave the question up to the employer.

### Sorry, the job's been filled...

You're bound to hear this line on occasion. Don't shrug your shoulders and say good-bye; perhaps other jobs are available that you would love every bit as much. If not, it's likely that there will be such openings one day. And there's always a chance that the person who got the job won't work out.

So request a meeting anyway. You could preface your request with, "I'm sorry to hear that I missed out on that opportunity. But I'm very interested in your company..." and so forth.

## Practice makes perfect

Effective salespeople rehearse their sales presentation until they have it down perfect. You should, too.

Write down your 60-second phone presentation, and try it out on a friend or family member. Then repeat it until you sound polished, but natural—you don't want to sound as if you're reading off a card. At the same time, stick close to your "script" so you don't forget important facts or wander away from the point.

Also, prepare for questions you may be asked during your follow-up call. Study your resume, and highlight points you may want to discuss if given the chance. Otherwise, you're liable to deliver a great 60-second spiel, but sputter about if further conversation develops.

## Learning to swim

Learning how to handle this phase of your job search requires time, effort and persistence. It's not easy. Selling anything involves a certain measure of rejection and disappointment—and when you're selling yourself, it's hard not to take the turndowns personally. But the more you do it, the better you will become.

Remember, you are offering to solve a company's problem. And keep in mind that the only way to get off your dead-end job shore is to start swimming.

# Chapter 16

# Closing the Sale: Interviewing

Congratulations! You landed that big job interview.

If you're like most of us, your initial euphoria over that coup is followed by major panic. What will you wear? What will you say? What if you blow it? What if you never get another chance like this in your life?

It's natural for you to be anxious. The outcome of the interview could very well change your life. But you need to get that anxiety under control so that the best *you* can shine through.

The secret to interview confidence—and success—is preparation. In this chapter, we'll look at some things you can do before, during and after the interview that will help you make a more effective marketing presentation.

## Do your research

As any salesperson will tell you, the first step in making a sale is getting to know the customer. The same is true when you want to sell yourself in a job interview. You must learn everything you can about the company so you can address issues that are important to the employer. The more you focus on those issues, the better you can convince the interviewer that you're the ideal solution to the company's problems.

Taking the time to research the company gives you another important advantage, too. It tells the employer that you're serious about the job and your career—a message that's more crucial than you might expect. Employers say that one of their biggest gripes about job applicants today is that too many arrive at the interview without any knowledge of the company's products, problems or competition.

You can't hope to convince an interviewer that you can meet the company's needs until you know what those needs are. So before your interview, do a little detective work and track down the answers to the following questions:

What are the company's major products and services?

Who are the company's customers?

- How do competitors and customers view the company? (Do they think the company's service is excellent or poor, that products are reasonably priced or a little too expensive?)

- What is the company's standing in the marketplace? Is it a profitable business, or is it teetering on the brink of bankruptcy?

- Who are the company's major competitors?

- What are some of the company's recent success stories?

- What are some potential problems the company may need to solve?

- Is the company privately or publicly owned? Is it an independent organization or part of a larger conglomerate?

- How big is the company? Has it grown or declined over the past five years? (Is it hiring or laying off people?)

In addition, you need to get a general idea of the company's corporate culture—a fancy term for "work environment." Is the environment casual? Steeped in tradition? Do people work under rigid rules and procedures, or are they encouraged to be more creative and independent? Do employees work together in project teams or does each person work alone?

Why are these issues important? Because it's difficult to accomplish much on the job when your approach to business clashes with the corporate norm. Your chances of moving up through the ranks aren't great, either. Employers today make a lot of noise about how much they value diversity in the workplace, but the reality is that those who conform to the company's ideas about work style, dress and professional ideology are the ones who get ahead.

To make sure that the corporate culture is one that would allow you to thrive, seek out the following information:

- Is the company "female-friendly?" (A good clue is the number of women in upper management.)

- Is it a relaxed, casual place to work or a very conservative, traditional office?

- Do employees work alone or in groups?

- Is the employee turnover rate high, average or low? What factors contribute to that turnover rate? (For example, do people leave the company because of low wages?)

- What type of employee is most valued? For example, do you need a certain college degree to move up the ranks or is on-the-job experience considered adequate training? Does the company smile upon risk-takers or prefer those who always follow company procedures to the letter?
- What is the overall corporate management philosophy?

Of course, you also need to find out as much as you can about the job itself. Some of the questions you'll want to research include:

- Why is the job available? Is it a new position? If not, why did the person who had the job leave?
- What are some of the problems you would be expected to solve if you were hired?
- What is the career path for people in this position? Do they usually move up the ladder or stay put?

# Where to look

To find the answers you need, you have several possible resources, and you should explore them all.

## 1. Call the company

First, call the company directly. Say that you're interested in learning more about the company and its products, and you'd like to see any annual reports, brochures or other materials that are available.

## 2. Visit the library

Next, head for the public library or the placement office at the nearest college or university. Read everything you can find about the company and the industry in general. Search through business magazines, newspapers and corporate reference books such as *Standard and Poor's Register of Corporations, Directors and Executives* and *Dun and Bradstreet's Million Dollar Directory*. If you're not familiar with these resources, ask the librarian for help.

## 3. Call your networking contacts

Ask your friends and other networking contacts if they know anyone who works for or does business with the company. When you turn up a good lead, call that person, introduce yourself and ask for a few minutes to chat about the company. This personal research is invaluable because you often learn things about the company that you'd never find in a published article or annual report.

### 4. Talk to your recruiter

If a search firm or employment agency arranged the interview for you, the recruiter should be able to answer many of your pre-interview questions. But don't depend on the recruiter as your sole source of information. It's possible that the employer wasn't entirely forthcoming in providing information to the recruiting firm, and it's also possible that the recruiting firm hasn't been entirely forthcoming with you.

## Collect references

Most employers today require job candidates to provide professional and/or personal references. Although most companies wait until the final phase of the hiring process to ask for references, some request them at the time of the first interview. The next step in your interview preparation, then, is to prepare a list of five or six people who might agree to provide you with references.

Your list could include former supervisors, teachers, volunteer-committee heads—anyone whose opinion employers will consider credible and objective. (This does not include a family member, however far removed!) Ideally, you should obtain references from people who are likely to be known as well as respected professionally by your potential employers. A word of warning: If you don't want your present employer to know about your job search, do not list fellow employees as references. However trustworthy, they may slip and let the cat out of the bag.

After you compile your list, ask people you've named if you can use them as references. You don't want them to be taken by surprise when a prospective employer calls.

## Interview day: the basics

### What to wear

Although it's true that appearances can be deceiving, you'll have a hard time convincing a prospective employer that you are a winner if you show up for your interview looking anything less than professional. So play it safe. Wear a fashionable business suit in a low-key color, a minimum of jewelry, simple accessories and low-heeled pumps. No low-cut or sheer blouses. No spike heels or sandals. No little-girlish jumpers and no mini-skirts or stretch pants.

Always dress as if you're interviewing for the CEO's job, no matter what position you're seeking. If you don't own an appropriate outfit, borrow or buy one. Yes, it's that important. Your appearance is the first thing an interviewer will notice—and that first impression is a lasting one.

If you work in one of the "creative" fields—advertising, art and the like—don't make the mistake of wearing your most avant-garde garb in an effort to show your creative genius. Let your portfolio do the talking in that regard. Your appearance should tell the interviewer that you also have a head for business.

Here's one more easy way to make points with an interviewer: Don't wear any cologne, perfume or other scent. When we asked hiring managers and HR specialists to name the biggest mistakes made by job applicants, about 90 percent ranked perfume-overkill high on the list. It's nearly impossible to tell how much is too much when it comes to perfume; what seems like a pleasant whiff of scent to you may overpower someone else. So why risk it? Save that Chanel No. 5 for another occasion.

## What to take

Pack a pencil and pen; your business cards, if you have any; the names, phone numbers and titles of your personal and professional references; and several copies of your resume. You may be interviewing with more than one contact at the company, and you want each one to have your resume. Your resume will also help guide you through the interview process and fill out an employment application, if you are asked to do so.

## Employment applications

Speaking of employment applications, be sure to fill them out completely, neatly and honestly. Make sure the information you put on your application matches that on your resume.

There is one section you should skip: requests for salary information. For reasons you'll learn in a few minutes, you don't want to disclose this information yet. Simply write "open" or "negotiable" or something similar.

## Be on time

Allow plenty of extra time to get to your interview; you never know when a traffic jam or other transportation catastrophe is going to occur. (Arriving early also gives you a chance to calm your nerves a bit before the interview begins.) If you run late because of some unavoidable problem, call ahead to let the interviewer know. Apologize profusely and ask whether the interviewer would prefer to reschedule.

### Remember that you're the guest

Interview etiquette says that you are the guest and the interviewer is the host. So don't sit down until the interviewer invites you to do so. Don't plop your briefcase down on the interviewer's desk, and don't start fingering any office knickknacks, even if it's one of those inviting little stress-relief gizmos. And if you think the wallpaper is tacky or the view of the parking lot is less than attractive, for heaven's sake don't say so.

### Don't smoke, chew gum or eat

Never light up a cigarette during an interview, even if the interviewer indulges in chain-smoking. Employers are very concerned about employee health today, and most people—even smokers—consider smoking to be a sign of poor health habits.

Don't have anything else in your mouth during the interview, either. That includes mints, gum and the rest of your soft drink from lunch. If the interviewer offers you a cup of coffee or other beverage, of course, feel free to accept if you're so inclined. But if you tend to be a klutz, it might be wise to reduce the risk of a mishap and turn down the offer.

### Be friendly to everyone you meet

Be at your professional best with *everyone* you meet, from the receptionist at the front door to the interviewer's secretary. There's a good chance that all of these people will be asked to offer an opinion about you. So treat every encounter as a "silent interview."

## How to answer interview questions

The next section presents some typical interview questions and suggestions on how to answer them. But regardless of what question you're asked, your response will be more effective if you keep the following tips in mind.

### Focus on accomplishments

Just as you did in your resume, tell the interviewer about specific accomplishments, not just your responsibilities. Whenever possible, provide qualitative information about the benefits your accomplishments brought. For example, say, "This increased company profits by 10 percent over a one-year period," rather than "This increased company profits."

## Don't be so modest

We talked in Chapter 1 about how women tend to be too modest, reluctant to toot their own horns. Be aware of this tendency in your own conversation, and guard against it. For instance, suppose that an interviewer compliments you on a particular accomplishment—graduating *cum laude*, for example. Don't say:

> *"Oh, thank you, but it was really nothing. The course work was fairly simple for me."*

Instead, say:

> *"Thank you. It was a challenge, because I was working part-time while carrying a full course load. But the experience helped me learn how to manage my time effectively."*

Such a statement not only confirms the interviewer's positive impression of you, it also points out that you succeeded in the face of challenge and defines the advantages of your experience.

## My manager says...

A great way to point up your skills without sounding too full of yourself is to say, "My supervisors have told me that I am very good at..." or "My clients will tell you that I..." This technique actually gives your statement added punch because you're telling the interviewer what other people think of you, not what you think of yourself.

## Be diplomatic and discreet

Never badmouth another employer, no matter how much you feel the urge. You'll only be viewed as a complainer or as someone who can't get along with others.

In addition, don't attempt to win favor with an interviewer by spilling the beans about your present employer's financial situation or offering up other confidential information, especially if you're interviewing with a competitor to your current employer. Interviewers will wonder if you'd be just as indiscreet with information their companies consider proprietary.

If you need to talk about financial accomplishments, you can do so without giving away company secrets. Instead of saying, "I brought in $3.5 million of the $49 million the company earned last year," you can just say, "I was responsible for 7 percent of the company's total sales last year."

## Help steer the interview

When you're the one being interviewed, you may feel nervous, at the interviewer's mercy. You need to realize that the interviewer may feel just as anxious.

Unless they do it on a daily basis, most people do not feel comfortable in the role of interviewer. In fact, if left to their own devices, many interviewers will spend the entire interview telling you about the job and never ask you any questions at all. Others get sidetracked on nonjob issues, spending your allotted interview time talking about hobbies, the weather, favorite restaurants, and so forth. Although such interviews can feel more relaxed and enjoyable, they can really hurt your chances of getting the position. Why? Because the interviewer never learns a thing about why you're the right person for the job.

If you find yourself in an interview that seems to be going nowhere, take the initiative to refocus the conversation on how your skills can solve the company's needs. Of course, you don't want to be so brash as to say something like, "Hey, don't you want to hear about my qualifications?" But you *can* give the interviewer a subtle push in the right direction. One good option is to open with a question, such as:

> *"I'd like to hear more about the quality control responsibilities that I'll be handling."*

After the interviewer describes those duties, you can then respond by explaining how you handled such tasks in past jobs:

> *"That sounds a lot like what I've done in my current position. Last fall, for example, I was responsible for developing a new quality-control system that helped us reduce customer complaints by 10 percent."*

# Sample interview questions

Every interviewer seems to have unique ideas about the best way to extract information from job candidates. You simply cannot predict exactly what questions you'll be asked in your interview. But here are

some of the most popular, along with some tips on how to an.
them effectively:

## "Tell me about yourself."

Vague, open-ended questions such as this one can get you in a lot of trouble. If you're not careful, you can end up telling interviewers more—or less—than they want to know.

Different interviewers ask this question (or a variation of it) for different reasons. One hiring manager may want to know about your current position, for example. Another may want to hear about your entire work history, starting with your very first job. Yet another may be interested in finding out about your personality and approach to business. It's important that you address the interviewer's real concern, so clarify the question by asking, "What aspects of my background are you specifically interested in hearing about?"

Be careful not to ramble on when you respond to this question. Even if interviewers say they want to hear the story of your life, make it a capsulized version. Many interviewees, especially women, get carried away and launch into a 10- or 15-minute discourse. Keep your answers short and to the point, remembering that the point always is, "What can you do for the company?"

## "What are your strengths and weaknesses?"

Interviewers ask this question not just to learn about your abilities and shortcomings, but also to find out how you see yourself—to see whether *you* think you've got what it takes to do the job.

Obviously, you want to identify as your strengths those skills or personality traits that seem most vital to the position. But what about that weaknesses bit? Do you really want to admit that you're lacking in some area? The answer is yes—and no. Don't say that you don't have any weaknesses; employers are extremely suspect of people who give that response. Instead, pick a weakness that: a) is low on the employer's list of required skills; and b) you're taking steps to correct. If you're applying for a managerial position, don't answer that your weakness is not being able to handle personnel conflicts well, for example. Better to mention your discomfort about having to speak to large groups and emphasize that you're going to your local Toastmaster's Club to improve your skills.

And don't spend a lot of time describing your weaknesses—you want to get off that subject as quickly as possible. Mention *one* weakness, explain how you are overcoming it, and then quickly shift the focus and start selling your strengths.

## "What are your accomplishments?"

When you're asked this question, emphasize accomplishments that are most relevant to the job. Suppose, for example, that you're interviewing for a job as a buyer in a department store. You have three years of experience as a retail-store manager, a degree in elementary education and four years experience as a child-care provider. From your company research, you know that the store is having problems because of poor relationships with suppliers. If the interviewer asks you to detail your current position, don't waste valuable interview time talking about your degree or your childcare experience—they're irrelevant to this position. Instead, talk up the vendor-relations experience and skills you gained as a store manager.

Be sure to stress how your accomplishment affected the company's bottom line in as specific terms as possible. It's also helpful to explain why you approached the project as you did. You need to show that you know how to assess a situation and plan a successful course of action.

Also mention any circumstances that made it more difficult for you to achieve your goal. For example, if you managed a department that met its sales quota during a period when your best producer was in the hospital, mention that and explain how you motivated the rest of the staff to pick up the slack. Often, what seems like a minor accomplishment at first glance is really a major achievement when you understand the circumstances under which it occurred.

## "Tell me about a failure."

When you answer this question, take responsibility for the failure and also explain what you learned from it. Interviewers want to know if you understand why you failed and know how to avoid similar problems in the future. You should also explain why you think the failure was significant. Doing so reflects an understanding of what's important in business and what's not.

Resist the urge to cite a poor economy, an idiot boss or miserable co-workers as the reason for your failure. Employers don't respect people who blame others for their troubles. They do respect people who have the courage to say, "I blew it, and here's why it will never happen again."

As with discussions about your weaknesses, don't spend too much time talking about your failures. Women, in particular, often overplay their failures and downplay their successes. Keep your answer brief and move quickly to a more positive subject. Try to follow up your failure story with an accomplishment that proves you learned your lesson.

## "Why do you want to work here?"

Interviewers ask this question to assess several things. First, they want to find out how much you know about the company. They also want to learn about your motivation. Do you want this particular job because of money? Because you heard that the company was a great place to work? Because you think you would enjoy the day-to-day responsibilities? Because you can't stand where you're at now and think any job would be an improvement?

Your goal is to assure the interviewer that you're not just after any old job, but that you chose this particular job and company because you think you can really contribute. You should also demonstrate that you've given careful thought to your career goals, because employers appreciate focused individuals.

Don't be phony or overly gushing—you don't have to say, "I think you're the very best company in the world and I don't want to work for anyone but you." But do let the interviewer know that you are excited about the possibility of being part of the organization.

If you're a displaced homemaker or are returning to the work force after raising a family, you may also have to answer a variation of the "Why do you want to work here" question. The interviewer may want to know why you want to work, period. This question usually is a sign that the interviewer thinks you may not be serious about a career. Your answer should assure the interviewer that your decision to work is not a whim, but a carefully researched and planned life goal.

## "Why are you leaving your job?"

Interviewers who ask this question want to know if you're leaving because you've been unable to succeed or fit in at your current company. They assume that if you have problems at your present company, you'll have problems at their company. They also may be interested in determining whether any of the issues that prompted you to leave your present position, such as salary, advancement opportunities and working conditions, exist in their company as well. If those issues do exist, they probably will eliminate you from further consideration, because they figure that you'll be just as unhappy in your new job as you were in your old one.

The best approach is to explain that you're running toward a new opportunity, not running away from a bad situation.

You can just say something to the effect of, "I've enjoyed a lot of success in my current job, but I'm ready for new challenges."

## "What are your career goals?"

Interviewers who ask this question do so not because they care so much about your personal happiness, but because they want to know whether you're likely to stay with the company for a while. They also want to know whether you really are interested in the job that's available or see it as a fast springboard to something better. Unless the company is actively looking for people they can move up quickly through the ranks, announcing that you want to be promoted within 12 months is a death wish. With the high cost of training and hiring employees today, interviewers are likely to cut you from the running if they think you won't be happy in the job for a reasonable amount of time.

When you define your career goals, try to find a middle ground between having no goals at all and having your life planned out down to the finest detail, all the way to retirement. You want to show that you do have some goals that are important to you and that the job in question fits nicely with those goals. But you also need to stress that your goals aren't written in stone—that you're always open to new opportunities.

## "What do you do for fun?"

This question is designed to help the interviewer assess your personality. Are you a workaholic, or do you have a good balance between your work and personal life? Are you someone who takes an active part in your community, or is your idea of community involvement limited to attending the local high school football games? If you are involved, do you participate in any activities that might prove embarrassing to the company?

You might think that the best answer to this question would be to say that you don't have any spare time because you work so hard at your job. Everybody wants a dedicated worker, right? Yes, to an extent. But employers today are also searching for well-balanced individuals who place equal importance on their personal and professional lives. They have learned that employees who spend 18 hours a day on the job very quickly burn out.

Just as you emphasize those skills and accomplishments that are most relevant to the position, mention those outside activities that are most likely to be positives in the interviewer's mind. Fitness activities are good bets because employers want healthy employees. Participation in professional trade groups is another winner because it shows that you have a keen interest in the industry. Volunteering in community activities also is a plus, but be careful: If you're a supporter of some political, religious or otherwise potentially controversial group, just don't bring it up. The interviewer just may be a member of the opposition.

### "So, do you have any questions?"

Many job applicants, in a rush to get out of the interview, don't ask any questions of the interviewer. That's a mistake.

Employers spend a lot of money hiring and training new employees. They want you to be sure the job is really a good fit before you sign on, because they know that if you're not happy on the job, you'll quit or be unproductive. Either way, they'll lose money. So don't be shy about asking for details you need to make an informed decision about whether the job is right for you. Most interviewers say that they are impressed when a candidate asks intelligent questions—and concerned when an interviewee doesn't ask any questions at all.

Choose your questions carefully, however. "What is your vacation policy?" or "How many single men work here?" are not the kind of questions an interviewer wants to hear. Stay away from questions about benefits or other personal issues.

What are some good questions to ask? Here are a few suggestions:

- What kind of orientation or training program will I complete when I begin the job?
- What kind of person succeeds in this company?
- What will be the biggest challenge I'll have in this job?
- What do you enjoy most about working for this company? What do you dislike most?

If you are interviewing with your prospective supervisor, consider these questions:

- Could you describe your management style?
- What are some goals you've set for this position for the coming year?
- Why did the person who had this job before succeed or fail?

## How to handle sticky situations

### Explaining career gaps

If you're one of the many women with gaps in employment history, you will have to address that. First, you need to assure the interviewer that you aren't planning on working for a year, then dropping out for another 10 (unless that is your plan, of course).

Second, you need to convince the interviewer that just because you've been out of the job market for a while, that doesn't mean that your skills are less than admirable. Here are a few suggestions on how to accomplish this.

**1. Position the gap as a career decision.** Let the interviewer know that your leave from the work force was a conscious decision about your life direction. This says that you are someone with a firm plan in mind. Perhaps:

> *"Yes, I chose to spend the last six years at home after my children were born. My plan was to continue with my professional career at the end of those six years because that is important to me as well as raising a family."*

**2. Focus on accomplishments and skills used during the gap.** Remind the interviewer of volunteer activities or personal accomplishments you mentioned on your resume. For example:

> *"Of course, during this time I handled many of the same responsibilities one faces on the job. For instance, I served as the chairperson of the PTA fund-raising committee for one year. I organized the committee, developed a mailing list of possible benefactors and coordinated a publicity drive. The campaign earned $15,000—a 15 percent increase over the previous year's effort."*

**3. Play up professional affiliations.** Be sure to mention your continued involvement with any professional or trade organizations related to your field. This lets the interviewer know that even though you've not been in the work force, you're still in touch with current industry issues and developments.

## Older, wiser—but never employed

Many women who have never been professionally employed find themselves in need of a job in their 30s, 40s or thereafter. If you're in this situation, you understand what an uphill battle the job search can be. You know you can handle the job, but employers can't seem to get past your nonexistent employment record.

For you, it's doubly important to dress, talk and act like the consummate professional during the interview. When mentioning volunteer or community activities, be sure to focus on specific tasks you performed.

Instead of saying:

*"I've been an active member of the Sunshine Hospital Volunteers for 15 years."*

Say:

*"From 1993 to 1994, I managed the budget for a city-wide hospital service organization. I collected dues from more than 200 members, kept formal accounting records, handled tax issues and developed the next year's budget. I'm proud to say that during that time, the organization earned 5 percent more interest on our savings funds because of banking decisions that I made."*

### "Have you ever been fired or laid off?"

Explaining a layoff or firing requires careful footwork. If you were let go because of corporate restructuring rather than for nonperformance, it's important to mention that fact. What if you were fired because of some gripe on the company's part? Keep in mind that potential employers probably will contact past employers to verify your credentials, at which point, the truth about whether you were fired or laid off will come out.

So don't lie, but don't reveal all the details, either. You might say something like, "Of course, I wasn't happy about being fired, but the job simply was not a good fit for me or for the company. So it was best for both of us in the long run that we part ways."

### "Hey baby, how about dinner?"

Although the world is becoming far less tolerant of such behavior, sexual harassment has not vanished from the interviewing office. So it is not out of the realm of the possible that you may find yourself on the receiving end of an interviewer's suggestive leer or, worse, hand.

What to do? If the interviewer is to be your direct supervisor or even department manager, the best choice is probably to grit your teeth, end the interview as soon as possible and scratch the position off your list. The situation is not likely to improve after you're on the job. Of course, you always have another option: to report the incident to the interviewer's higher-up, if there is one.

If you're really interested in the company, you may want to investigate job possibilities in other departments. Then again, you may want to think twice about a company that permits such behavior in any of its personnel.

## "Are you a family woman?"

The law forbids employers from basing hiring decisions on your marital or family status. That doesn't stop most employers from asking about these issues. You don't have to answer, of course. But where will that get you? Out the door, most likely. Let's say that the employer does mean to discriminate. If you refuse to answer, the interviewer will assume that you're "one of those women's libbers" or that you won't answer because you do in fact have family conflicts that might hinder your job performance. Either way, your defiance will be a big black mark against you.

Now let's suppose that your interviewers are simply ignorant of the law. Should you enlighten them? Well, if you did, they're likely to either become embarrassed or defensive—and neither emotion is conducive to building your interview rapport.

It's no secret that many employers believe that women who are wives and mothers miss work frequently, are reluctant to travel and often quit to follow their husbands to a new job location. So if you are a wife or a mother or both, how do you answer questions about your family status without damaging your chances for the job? By keeping the employer's true concerns in mind.

Questions about your family life really represent a hidden objection. The interviewer doesn't really care that you have a loving husband or that you've chosen to have children—your lifestyle isn't the issue. The issue is whether your lifestyle will affect your ability to do the job in any way. Which means that the best way to answer such questions is to say something on the order of the following:

> *"Yes, I do have two children. I have great childcare arrangements, too, so you don't have to worry that my family might interfere with my work. We even have a backup plan in place so that if our regular caregiver is sick, I don't have to miss work to be with the kids."*

or:

> *"Yes, I do have a family, but I make it a point not to let that interfere with my work. In fact, at my last job, I never missed one day because of family problems or sick children."*

If the interviewer really starts to focus on your personal life, you can usually put a halt to it with a simple statement such as:

> *"You know, I sense that you're concerned about whether my personal life will keep me from performing well. I can assure you that this has not been the case in the past and it won't be so in the future. Now that we've got that resolved, what other questions can I answer for you?"*

This same approach is effective when interviewers ask other types of discriminatory questions, too. Just for the record, the law restricts employers from basing hiring decisions on your age, ancestry or race, as well as on many aspects of your personal life, including your religion and your sexual orientation.

# After the interview

An interview is hard, stressful work. So the first thing to do when you walk out of the interviewer's office is to relax a bit! But then, there are a few important follow-up measures to take.

## Write a thank-you note

Always write a brief thank-you note. Thank the interviewer for taking the time to meet with you, and restate your interest in the company and position. Try to incorporate mention of some part of the interview—ideally, a particular need the interviewer expressed and how you might address that need. But keep your letter to one or two short paragraphs. Type the letter in business style, and be sure there are no typos or spelling errors. Look at the following sample:

---

Dear Ms. Kranz:

Thank you for taking the time to discuss the position of store manager with me yesterday. It was a pleasure meeting you and learning more about Eversman's Pharmacy.

During our meeting, you mentioned that you'll be shopping around for a new computerized inventory system soon. I've been recalling my own experience with inventory systems at Webber Drugs, and I have a few ideas about which systems might work best for you. I'd be happy to share my thoughts with you at any time.

Again, thank you for your consideration. I look forward to hearing from you and to the possibility of joining your staff.

Sincerely,

---

If you were able to arrange the interview because of a tip or personal introduction from a colleague or networking contact, be sure to drop that person a note of thanks as well.

### Evaluate the interview

Replay the interview in your mind. What went well? What could you have done better? The point is not to berate yourself for what you did or didn't say; you did the best job you knew how. The point is to determine which things worked and which didn't, and to use that knowledge in your next interview.

### Study your resume again

Did the interviewer have any questions about information on your resume—questions that could be clarified by a slight rewrite? Did you find yourself mentioning important accomplishments or skills that you neglected to put on your resume? If so, you should revise your resume accordingly.

### When to call back

Especially in corporate America, the hiring process moves at an amazingly slow pace. So don't panic if a week or two passes and you don't hear anything from your interviewer. No news may indeed be good news.

During your interview, make it a point to ask when the hiring decision will be made. If you don't get word about the job by that time, it's perfectly acceptable to call the employer to inquire about the status of the position. If the job has not yet been filled, you can use the opportunity to remind the employer of your interest and your qualifications.

Don't, however, be a pest. If they're not ready to make a decision, they're not ready to make a decision.

# Chapter 17

# Negotiating Your Best Deal

You just heard those magical, marvelous words: "We'd like you to work for us." Now it's time to close the sale and get the best price for your product—in other words, to negotiate the terms of your salary and benefits package.

If you're like most people, this part of the job hunt provokes a lot of anxiety. You want to get the best compensation package you possibly can, but at the same time, you're afraid that if you ask for more than the employer initially puts on the table, the job offer might be withdrawn. You may be tempted to snap up whatever the employer offers just to avoid all those uncomfortable feelings that crop up during the negotiation process.

That's fine—as long as the employer is offering you a fair wage. Take the money and run, as they say. But if you accept a salary or benefits package that's less than it should be, you'll hurt yourself not only financially, but emotionally. You'll soon come to resent the employer for paying substandard wages, and that anger can't help but reduce your job satisfaction. You owe it to yourself—and to the employer—to work out a deal that satisfies you both.

Yes, salary negotiation is a tricky prospect. You can indeed damage your relationship with the employer if you go about negotiations in the wrong way—maybe even to the point that the employer decides that hiring you isn't such a good idea after all. But if you follow a few basic negotiation rules and strategies, you should be able to agree on a compensation that will leave you and the employer feeling good about your new partnership.

## Know your worth

The first key to successful salary negotiation is research. Before you discuss salary, you need to know the going rate for the job. You also must know how much employers in your area are paying people with your level of experience, education and skill. Without this information, you have no way of knowing whether the employer is offering you a fair market price for your services.

In Chapter 3, we advised you to research compensation levels for jobs in your chosen field. If you don't already know the salary range for the specific position you're considering, dig up the data you need now. Don't forget to look at average salary levels for your city and state, not for the entire country.

Also determine whether the figures you see reflect salary alone or include the value of insurance plans, retirement programs and other employee benefits. And pay attention to whether you're looking at salaries earned by men or women! Remember, in most cases, women still earn less than men doing the same job. You should request, and expect to earn, the same salary paid to a similarly qualified man.

## Don't negotiate until an offer is made

Never enter into salary negotiations until the employer makes you a firm job offer. At that point, you're in your strongest negotiating position because you know that the company has decided that you're the best candidate for the job.

If the interviewer asks you during your first meeting how much money you expect, try dodging the question. You want the employer to name a figure first, if at all possible. Why? Because otherwise, you may state a salary that's lower than what the employer is willing to pay, thereby cheating yourself out of hundreds or thousands of dollars a year. Or you might suggest a salary figure that's higher than what the employer had in mind, in which case the company may think it can't afford you and put your resume into the "not available" pile. Either way, you lose.

When an interviewer asks you what salary you want, you can sidestep the question saying something like:

> *"I need to know a little more about the job responsibilities and the level of expertise you're expecting before I can suggest an appropriate salary."*

If you're pressed to name your salary expectations, don't refuse, but don't commit yourself to a specific figure. Instead, offer a salary range:

> *"I expect a fair market wage, of course. I believe that for this position, the going rate in this area is in the $25,000-to-$35,000 range."*

Always give a fairly broad range to minimize the chances that you will be way under or way over the salary the employer has allotted for the job. The bottom figure should be the minimum you will accept.

## How much can you negotiate?

Some companies have rigid salary structures in place and don't allow any negotiation at all. Some establish a salary range for each position and give the hiring manager or HR director latitude to negotiate within that range. Others don't have any firm salary rules and may agree to a higher compensation package if they think the candidate is worth the extra expense.

Generally, the higher up the corporate ladder you go, the more you can bargain for added wages, benefits and perks. Usually, employers don't negotiate salaries for entry-level, hourly positions.

Your negotiation power also is affected by the job market. If there are a lot of people on the market with your same skills and level of experience, you obviously won't have as much leverage as someone with qualifications that are hard to find. Employers know that if you don't take the job, someone else will.

However, don't assume that just because the job market is crowded or the position isn't an executive-level one that you can't negotiate at all. Remember, the employer selected you as the best applicant for the job, so you must have something the others don't.

If you ask for a higher salary or a few more benefits in the right way—and your request is reasonable—you won't risk losing the offer. You can always lower your asking price if need be. And the employer just may surprise you and agree to your request.

## Make your best deal now

Your best—and sometimes only—opportunity to negotiate a higher salary is *before* you join a company. After you're on the job, it will be very difficult to increase your compensation substantially because any raises you receive will be based on your starting salary.

In most companies today, the average annual raise is in the neighborhood of 3 to 5 percent. Some employers won't raise your salary much more than that—even when they give you a promotion. If you work for such an employer, you'll be lucky if a promotion nets you an increase of 10 to 15 percent. You can see, then, how critical it is that you negotiate your best deal when you accept a new job.

# How to respond to a job offer

When an employer makes you a job offer, the first thing you need to do is determine whether the terms of the deal meet your needs or whether you need to negotiate for a higher salary or better benefits. The way you respond to the employer's initial offer can make a difference in the outcome of any later negotiations, so step lightly and carefully.

## 1. Express your enthusiasm

First, tell the employer that you're pleased and excited to have been selected. Enthusiasm is catching, and you want the employer to remain enthusiastic about you during the negotiation process. Telling the employer how pleased you are about the opportunity also sets a positive climate for any subsequent negotiations.

## 2. Ask for time to think it over

Never accept a job offer on the spot. You'll be too focused on the excitement of getting the offer to make a clear-headed decision. Take at least 24 hours to consider the offer—more, if possible.

If the salary is substantially lower than you can accept, give some indication of that when the offer is made. A good way to do this is to say something like the following:

> *"I've been very impressed with your company and I'd really like to work with you. I'm going to consider your offer very carefully, but I do want to let you know that the salary is a bit below what I had in mind. As I think about this, it would make me feel more comfortable if I knew there might be some flexibility in the compensation package."*

By making this statement right away, you let the employer know that some salary negotiation is necessary. The hiring manager or the HR person handling the negotiation can then begin getting any necessary approvals to raise the salary level or look for other ways to sweeten the pot, such as offering a sign-on bonus or additional benefits.

If the employer tells you that no flexibility is possible, you know before you consider the offer that the salary package isn't likely to be improved. It's always possible that the employer is bluffing at this point, or that you'll be able to convince the employer to become flexible later on in the negotiation. But at the very least, you're forewarned that getting an increase in the offer will be difficult.

If the salary you're offered is higher than you expected, don't let on and don't rush to accept the job. This situation also calls for some careful consideration. It could be that you've underestimated your value on the market or that there's something about the position you neglected to take into account when you came up with your salary range.

## 3. Ask for details

If the employer does not provide them, ask for details about non-wage compensation—insurance benefits, paid vacation days and other perks that add value to the offer. You can say:

> *"As I'm considering your offer, it will help me to know about any benefits that I would receive in addition to salary. Can we please go over those now, or do you have any literature that explains them?"*

Alternatively, you can ask for the name of the appropriate person in HR who can discuss these issues with you. Among the basic benefits you should inquire about are:

- **Health, dental, life and disability insurance.** Ask for specifics about coverage, especially for health insurance. Deductibles, benefit limits and other features vary widely from employer to employer and can make a significant impact on the total value of the compensation package.

- **Retirement or pension plans.** Find out whether the employer matches employee contributions to such plans and how long it takes to become vested in the plan (the number of years you must work at the company before you are entitled to your funds).

- **Overtime policies.** Will you be paid on an hourly basis, offered extra days off as compensation or be expected to work overtime with no additional pay? Do these policies apply to days you spend traveling on company business?

- **Profit-sharing plans.**

- **Vacation days and sick days.**

- **Tuition reimbursement** for training related to your job.

- **Employee discounts** on company products.

Depending upon the position, you may also want to inquire about the following:

- **A company car** or a car maintenance and gas allowance (for jobs involving automobile travel).
- **A termination contract** that specifies a certain severance payment if you're laid off before a set period of time (usually reserved for executive positions).
- **Stock options** (if the company is a publicly traded firm).
- **Moving expenses** (if the job requires relocation).

Also, be sure to ask how and when the company awards raises to employees. Find out what you can reasonably expect in terms of annual increases and whether those increases are based on performance or simply on cost-of-living factors. If the company does reward employees based on performance, ask how your performance will be evaluated.

## 4. Evaluate the offer

When you assess the employer's offer, look at the big picture. Don't think just about base salary, but about the value of the total compensation package. Consider, too, whether the compensation will be acceptable to you in the future as well as today, given what you learned about the employer's pattern of wage increases.

Don't forget to factor in any expenses associated with the job. For example:

- How much money will you spend commuting to the job?
- If you have young children, how much will you spend on day care while you're at work?
- If you're moving to take a job, is the cost of living in the new location higher or lower than where you live now?

In addition to analyzing the offer in monetary terms, evaluate how much personal and professional satisfaction you will get from the job:

- Does the job fit in with your long-term career plans?
- Do you have a reasonable chance of being successful?
- How many hours will you be spending on the job?
- What, if anything, are you giving up if you take the job?
- Will you enjoy the corporate culture, and is it one that values individuals like you?

One word of caution: Some employers, in an effort to convince you to take the job, promise future rewards. They may tell you, for example, that they plan to expand in the next two years and imply that if you come on board now, you'll be the first to head up a new division when the expansion occurs. Take all of this into consideration, but don't agree to work for less than fair market value today in exchange for future benefits unless you're absolutely certain that you'll be paid back in full for your efforts. There's no guarantee that the employer will be willing or able to keep promises made to you.

### 5. Accept, decline or negotiate

If, after careful assessment of these issues, you decide you do want the job and the compensation seems appropriate, you may choose to accept the offer as is. Call the employer and say that you are delighted to accept the position.

If you decide that you don't want the job, no matter what the salary, turn down the position politely and professionally. Don't forget that although this particular job might not be right for you, you may want to be considered for future openings. So be very gracious in your rejection of the offer.

If the offer is lower than you'd like and/or you think the employer may be willing to bump up the compensation a bit, it's time to plot and prepare your negotiating strategy.

## Negotiating a better deal

Before you respond to the employer's offer and start the negotiation process, determine the minimum package of salary and benefits you will accept in exchange for your services. Then create a "wish list" of the salary, benefits or perks you'd like to get over and above your bottom line. This is the compensation package you'll request at the beginning of your negotiation.

How much should you ask for? A little more than you think you can get. Shoot above the employer's target salary with the goal of working toward a middle ground that satisfies you both. Include on your wish list some benefits you're willing to concede, so the employer "wins" on those points.

However, be sure that your requests are reasonable given the market value of the position and your qualifications. If your requests are too much above the norm, you'll look foolish, uninformed or not serious about taking the job.

Whatever you do, don't try to justify a higher salary based on your personal financial needs. Sure, you may be concerned about whether you'll be able to cover the mortgage payment, your health club membership, the new car and day-care costs. But that's not the employer's problem! Focus your discussion on the market value of the position and the skills and experience you will be bringing to the company.

When you have determined your bottom line and created your wish list, you're ready to call the employer and kick off the negotiating process with a statement such as:

> *"I've thought carefully about your offer, and I want to repeat that I'm very interested in joining the company. However, I do have some concerns about the compensation package that I'd like to discuss with you."*

Then work your way through your wish list until you're satisfied with the deal. While you're negotiating, remember that your objective is to get what you want and, at the same time, continue building a good relationship with the employer. So throughout the process, always maintain a positive, cooperative attitude. Be firm in your requests, but approach the negotiation from a win-win standpoint, letting the employer know that you want to work out a solution that will be good for both parties.

## How to get past common salary objections

When you ask for more than an employer initially offers, it's likely that you'll encounter some resistance. Most employers will try to convince you to bring your price down, just as you'll try to convince them to raise their offer.

Employers typically cite a few standard reasons for not wanting to increase the compensation package. Let's look at these objections and some strategies you can use to overcome them.

**1. "That's more than we allocated for the job."** Your first strategy in this situation, obviously, is to convince the employer to revise the budget allocation for the position. To do that, you'll have to help the employer realize that the salary is below market value. It's important to make your case politely and without a trace of resentment or annoyance. Emphasize your interest in the job again, and then address the issue of fair market value:

> *"This position does sound perfect to me, but the salary level the company has established is below what other employers in the area are paying. Although I would really like to work for you, I can't justify doing so for less than market rate, which is $21,000 to $27,000."*

**2. "You'd be earning more than others at that level."** When you hear this objection, you can try one of two responses. The first is to persuade the employer that you should earn more because you're worth more. If you know, for example, that you have a more advanced college degree or more experience than others in the department, you can point that out as evidence of the additional value you'll bring to the company.

The second option is to suggest that you be given a different job title so that you fall in a higher salary range. You can suggest that you assume a few additional responsibilities to compensate for the higher salary. Understand, though, that this won't be an easy battle to win, especially in a large, very structured company. Employers don't like to fool with job titles and salary levels once they are assigned. Generally, you will have a better shot at getting a job title changed if the company is smaller and does not use a formal pay-grade structure.

**3. "That's all our budget will allow."** The company may very well be unable to provide you with a higher salary. If you think that the employer is being sincere about budget constraints, negotiate for noncash benefits. For example, suggest that you'll accept the lower salary in exchange for a few hours off each week or for additional vacation days.

However, try to get some indication of when the employer expects the budget to improve. If there's not enough money to pay you market value now, there might not be enough next year, either. But if the employer expects a major turnaround soon, you may want to negotiate for future compensation. Suggest that the two of you set specific performance goals for your first six months or year on the job and that you be awarded a certain bonus or salary increase if you meet those goals.

**4. "That's too much more than your last salary."** Some employers try to base salary offers on how much you made in your last job. You must help the employer realize that your current or past salaries are irrelevant because the value of your last job has nothing to do with the value of the new job. You can say something like:

*"You're right—I did earn substantially less on my last job. However, keep in mind that I've been in that job for three years, and the experience I've gained over that time certainly warrants an increase."*

Here's another alternative:

*"I am paid much less at my current job than you're offering. However, as you're probably aware, I am underpaid in that position; the employer isn't paying market rates. Because that's one of the reasons why I'm considering leaving my current job, I wouldn't want to accept anything less than market value for a new job."*

**5. "You've been out of the work force for a while."** If you're trying to break back into the working world after several years of unemployment, you may find that some employers expect you to work for less because of your absence. The logic, presumably, is that you won't be as productive as other employees because you'll need some retraining. Employers may also assume that you are desperate for a job because you haven't worked for awhile.

You must prove that you offer the same skills as others with your same level of experience and therefore are worth full market value. You might ask the employer what skills you would need to earn market rate. Then you can remind the employer that you do offer those skills by pointing to your volunteer activities or other experience.

If that doesn't work, you can say that you'll take the lower salary with the understanding that your performance will be reviewed in six months. Ask the employer to agree that if you meet specific performance criteria—thereby proving that you're equally adept as everyone else with the same job title—your salary will be increased to the going market rate.

**6. "I'm sorry, but it's our policy not to negotiate."** This is a tough one, because you must determine whether the employer is really being truthful. If you know from your networking contacts or other research that the employer's policy prevents salary negotiation, you probably shouldn't push your luck. But if you think that the employer may be willing to give a little, you can say:

*"I understand that you don't normally negotiate on the issue of salary. But I think that you may agree that an exception is warranted in this case, because..."*

Explain why the salary is not appropriate for the position and restate your salary request. Again, if the employer can't negotiate base salary, ask for non-cash benefits to build the compensation package to an acceptable level.

# Know when to quit

At some point in your negotiation, the employer will say that the company has reached its maximum offer. If you think that the employer may be bluffing, test your theory by saying politely:

*"I'd like to think over this offer tonight and give you an answer tomorrow. However, I think it's only fair to let you know that some compensation issues are still a concern to me. Before I make my decision, is there anything else we can do to resolve these issues?"*

If the answer is no, accept the fact that the employer is either unable or unwilling to raise the compensation package further. Keep pushing beyond this point, and you'll annoy and anger the employer, possibly to the extent that the offer is withdrawn.

## Should you accept a low offer?

Only you can answer that question. You must determine whether other aspects of the position, such as advancement potential, working conditions or job satisfaction, outweigh a salary offer that's less than it should be. If you do decide to accept the position, however, be sure that you can go into the job with a good attitude. If you feel any resentment about having to work for less than you wanted, you should probably decline the offer. A salary issue that bothers you now will frustrate you even more after you're on the job.

## Solidify the deal

When you and the employer come to an agreement over salary and benefits, write a brief letter outlining the terms of the deal. Verbal agreements have a way of being ignored or forgotten after the negotiation is through. When you have a written document that details your agreement, on the other hand, it's more difficult for the employer to fudge on the terms later on.

Some employers make it a policy to send letters of agreement to all new hires, but in most cases, putting the deal in writing will be up to you. It's better to take on this task yourself than to ask the hiring manager or HR staff member to do it for you—they likely won't appreciate having to do more work on your behalf.

Unless you're taking an executive-level position, in which case you might want to consider having a lawyer draft a formal employment contract, this letter of agreement needn't be long or complicated. Begin the letter by restating your excitement about the offer, and then say something like, "To make sure that I haven't misunderstood any terms of our agreement, I've outlined the major points below." Then briefly list the base salary, benefits and perks the employer agreed to give you. Include any agreements about your job title, starting date and special performance bonuses (state the specific goals you're expected to meet along with the rewards you'll earn if you achieve those goals). Also note briefly your understanding of how and when your salary and performance will be reviewed.

Next, say that if you don't hear from the employer, you'll assume that your letter represents the agreement properly. (This relieves the employer of the chore of sending a formal response if everything is in order.) End the letter by emphasizing again that you're looking forward to being part of the company.

# Don't look back

Most people have a strange reaction after they accept a job offer. They're elated initially, but they soon start having second thoughts.

You'll probably experience the same doubts when you say yes to a new job. You may wonder whether you'll really like the work. You may question whether you should have asked for more money. You may be nervous about trying to fit in someplace new or taking on the new challenges.

These feelings are entirely natural. After all, your life is about to change. But don't let fears of the unknown spoil your excitement or, worse, convince you to turn back. You've made an informed, carefully thought-out decision, so celebrate your success and forge ahead on your new adventure. The same strength, smarts and savvy that helped you emerge victorious from a very difficult job hunt will enable you to be just as successful on the job.

# Chapter 18

# Keep Your Chin Up

Looking for a job is a tough business. It's full of pressure and rejection. And when things don't go the way you'd planned, when that hoped-for interview falls through or someone else gets the job you wanted, it's easy to get down on yourself, to give up.

Fight that urge with everything you've got. Don't indulge in self-criticism, telling yourself that you'll never find a job, that you're not as qualified or as smart or as skilled as other people. Those little voices in your head are powerful forces, and if you allow them to start making negative comments, pretty soon you'll begin believing what they have to say. And if you think you're a failure, you increase the odds that you will fail.

Tell yourself that you're a winner, however, and you'll find ways to succeed, no matter what. So when job-search setbacks occur—as they inevitably will—don't attack yourself. Instead, review your situation from an objective viewpoint, and look for ways to fix whatever might be going wrong. And learn to be your own best cheerleader! If a friend were in your shoes, you'd be full of encouraging words, wouldn't you? Say those words to yourself, and take them to heart.

We know: Easier said than done. But the following "Top 10 Tips for Frustrated Job Seekers" will help you silence those critical inner voices and concentrate with renewed energy on finding your ideal job.

## 1. Don't take rejection personally

Hiring is a business decision, pure and simple. Just because an employer didn't offer you a particular position doesn't mean you're unlikable or undesirable as an employee. It simply means that this employer, at this time, felt that someone else was a closer match for the job.

Remember, too, that there are some aspects of the employment game you simply can't control. It's very possible that the reason you didn't get the job had absolutely nothing to do with you. Perhaps the hiring manager had a fight with his wife right before your interview. Maybe the interviewer really wanted to hire you—but the company owner opted to give a favorite niece the position. You would have made a great employee; the company lost out.

## 2. Look at how far you've come

Take out your resume. No, not to work on it again. Just to read it. Who is that woman it describes? Who is that go-getter who achieved all of those things? Who learned to make such an impressive marketing statement? That's you.

Your resume is not only a powerful job-search tool, it's a great ego booster. Tack it up on your bulletin board or make room for it among the kids' school papers on the refrigerator door. If those negative voices start up, a look at your resume will remind you of all you have accomplished and all you have to offer.

## 3. Turn setbacks into learning experiences

On her very first job interview after graduating from college, one of the authors of this book received some unsolicited advice regarding her resume. The interviewer gently suggested that it would be best if she removed the part that explained that she left a previous job because the boss was incompetent.

The other author, several years into her career and considering herself quite a sophisticated professional, found herself not to be quite as skilled at interviewing as she imagined. When asked during a job interview whether she would mind tending the office coffee pot for the men in the office (because that was the woman's role in the office, dear), she was so taken aback that she blurted out, "I can't believe you just asked me that! How sexist can you be!"

We share these embarrassing moments with you to emphasize the following point: Experience is a wonderful teacher. The more interviews you go on, the more cover letters and resumes you write, the better you'll become at selling yourself. So view each interview or job application as an educational opportunity. Even if you don't walk away with the job, you'll win, because you'll gain knowledge you can use to make your next presentation even stronger.

## 4. Ask for employer input

You had a great interview. You thought you answered every question just right, and the hiring manager seemed to like you. Yet you didn't get the job. Instead of curling up in defeat, try to find out why you weren't selected. Call the hiring manager, and in a polite, sincere manner, ask what specific skills or experience you are lacking. Also ask for comments about your resume or interviewing skills. This feedback will help you learn how you might do better the next time.

Most people will be flattered that you asked for their input, as long as you request it in the right way. Don't try to change the hiring manager's mind, insist that you are better qualified than the candidate chosen or act annoyed about criticism you hear. Listen to what's being said, and understand that even if you don't think the remarks are valid, they reveal a lot about how you are being perceived.

Write a brief note to thank the individual for this advice. You want to stay in good graces so you'll be considered for future openings. Possibly, the employer may even steer you toward a similar position at another company in town.

## 5. Review your strategy

If you're not having any luck at all—your inquiries go unanswered, you can't get an interview, or your interviews lead to dead ends—take another look at your approach. Are you going after jobs that you are under- or overqualified to do? Is your resume lacking in looks or content? Are you targeting companies that don't need your services? Rethink, and if necessary, refocus your marketing campaign to address these problems.

## 6. Get an objective opinion

You may be so close to your job search that you can't see things clearly. Discuss your resume, your cover letters and your interview responses with a professional ally or a trusted mentor. Ask for suggestions on what you might change to improve the response you get from employers. You may even want to do some role-playing, having your friend ask you typical interview questions so the two of you can evaluate and refine your answers.

## 7. Change your situation

If you keep hearing that you lack required experience or skills, take steps to correct that situation. Sign up for a night class. Take on a volunteer position that allows you to acquire experience in a certain area. Look for projects you can tackle in your present job that offer a chance to generate some solid accomplishments.

Don't put your job search on hold while you're doing all of this, though. You can mention your current undertakings on your resume and stress to interviewers that you are acquiring more experience or education in a certain area.

## 8. Broaden your circle of friends

Keep in mind that it's usually not what you know, but who you know that will get you the job. So go out of your way to make new acquaintances, and don't be shy about networking. Join a club, or volunteer to work on community projects. Actually *attend* one of those trade association luncheons you somehow never have time for. Find out who's hiring, and ask for an introduction.

## 9. Seek out new resources

There are hundreds of nonprofit organizations dedicated to helping people find jobs, including many devoted solely to serving women with special needs. You'll find a listing of some of these groups at the end of this book, and there are sure to be others in your area.

Take advantage of these resources! The insights and assistance they provide can be invaluable, and generally there is little or no cost to you.

## 10. Be good to yourself

Instead of chastising yourself for losing out on an opportunity, pat yourself on the back for those positive steps you do take. Did you send out a resume today? Work on a cover letter? Follow up on a job lead? Respond well to a tough interview question? Treat yourself to a little reward. It doesn't have to be expensive—spend half an hour sipping an espresso in your favorite coffee shop, make yourself a good dinner, have a picnic in the park with your kids. Do all those nice little things for yourself that you would do to bolster the spirits of a friend or mate.

## You can do it!

The right job for you is out there. It may take some time to find it, but find it you will. Give yourself the credit you deserve, and don't get discouraged. Never forget: You're one smart woman. And a smart woman gets what she wants.

# Job-Search Resources

You are not alone. Whether you're a displaced homemaker or a professional seeking a boost in your career, there are associations, networks, agencies, publications and references out there to assist you on your job-search journey. Following are a mere handful of such services available:

## Agencies and organizations offering job-search assistance

**National Displaced**
**Homemakers Network**
1625 K Street NW
Suite 300
Washington, DC  20006
202-467-6346

This grant-funded program supports 1,100 regional programs that offer individual career counseling, as well as workshops on career planning, job hunting and self-esteem. Membership is $15 and includes a newsletter, "Network News," mailed four times a year, which features occupation information and more. Call for the center nearest you.

**AARP WORKS**
601 E Street NW
Washington, DC  20049
202-434-2277

Located in 90 communities nation-wide, AARP-sponsored workshops are targeted to women age 50 or older. The workshops assist job-seekers in assessing their skills, determining career direction and mounting a job search. There is a nominal charge for the workshops. Call AARP WORKS at the above phone number for information on the program nearest you.

**kiNexus**
640 North LaSalle St., Suite 560
Chicago IL  60610
800-828-0422

Endorsed by the National Association of Female Executives (NAFE), this information service provides an opportunity for job-hunting subscribers to get their names out to hundreds of companies and hiring managers nationwide. For a small fee ($30, or $20 for students), your "electronic resume" will be added to the kiNexus database for one year. Companies that tap into the data-base range from AT&T to Lord & Taylor, and experience requirements include entry-level and up. Most positions do require either post-secondary education or some years of experience in the field. Call the toll-free number and you'll receive a resume form to complete and return.

**Women's Wire**
1820 Gateway Dr.
San Mateo, CA  94404
415-378-6500

This commercial online service provides information about topics of interest to women, from spousal abuse to women's health issues to job and career concerns. Members can communicate via e-mail, open forums, private chats and scheduled conferences. There's a monthly service charge of $9.95.

**Forty Plus of New York**
15 Park Row
New York, NY  10038
212-233-6086
Fax: 212-227-2974

The 21 Forty Plus organizations across the country, each operating independently, offer help to out-of-work women and men over 40 who've previously been employed in management or in a professional occupation. Membership includes a comprehensive job-hunt campaign package, consisting of career counseling, assistance with resume writing, networking tips, interviewing skills and more. Members have access to Forty Plus facilities, which include word processing, computer and office support. And best of all, members can count on the expertise, advice and support of their peers. Membership fees vary for each organization. Call Forty Plus of New York for information on the center nearest you.

**American Women's Economic Development Corporation (AWED)**
71 Vanderbilt Avenue, 3rd Fl.
New York, NY 10169
212-688-1900
800-222-AWED

For the woman who is a business owner or who's decided to work for herself, this service offers counseling and advice, either one-to-one in-house or over the phone. For those who live in the New York area, there are also workshops on starting up a business, managing a business and more. A $55 annual membership fee helps reduce costs for workshops and counseling services. All counseling, however, is done on appointment-basis only. Call to schedule, or for more information.

**American Business Women's Association**
9100 Ward Parkway, Box 8728
Kansas City, MO 6414
816-361-6621

Throughout the country, 1,800 local groups provide opportunities for women to help themselves and others grow personally and professionally. The groups provide networking support, resume services, loan programs and more.

**National Association for Female Executives**
30 Irving Pl., 5th Fl.
New York, NY 10011
212-645-0770
800-927-6233

More than 200 local affiliates provide networking opportunities for women in business. NAFE also offers career-oriented conferences and seminars, a career data bank, a resume guide and writing service.

## Resources in your library reference section

**Business Organizations and Agencies Directory.** Gale Research Co.
This directory lists businesses, nationwide, by name, type of activity, location and more. Includes name, address and phone number of organizations, and frequently lists a contact name.

**Contacts Influential.** Contacts Influential America, a division of American Business Information.

This directory series covers 20 regions throughout the U.S. and includes information on large and smaller businesses. Names, addresses, phone numbers, contact names, number of employees and descriptions are included. To find out whether there's a directory covering your area, call 402-593-4578.

**Encyclopedia of Associations.** Gale Research Co.

This lists thousands of associations, cross-referenced by name, location and type of association. Includes names, addresses, phone numbers and descriptions, membership base, publications and more. A great source for networking.

**Million Dollar Directory.** Dun & Bradstreet.

More than 150,000 businesses in a range of industries are listed. Each listing includes information such as the address, phone number, names and titles of top management, and other pertinent data about the company.

**Standard & Poor's Register of Corporations, Directors and Executives.** Standard & Poor's Corp.

More than 40,000 corporations, cross-referenced by names, types of business and location are listed. Includes names and titles of key executives and management.

# Feedback, please

Writing a book about job hunting is almost (but not quite) as difficult as hunting for a job. There's never enough room to include everything and answer all the questions, and there are undoubtedly topics that we didn't cover.

If you have any comments, suggestions or recommended additions, please write to us at Career Press, 3 Tice Rd., P.O. Box 687, Franklin Lakes, NJ 07417. Your input will be invaluable as we go to write the next edition of *The Smart Woman's Guide to Resumes and Job Hunting*.

# Index

Aburdene, Patricia, 18
Accessories, for the
    interview, 175
Accomplishments, 27-28, 34-36,
    68, 110, 134, 176-177, 180, 184
Ads
    blind, 156-157
    classified, 22, 155-157
Affiliations, 118-119
    professional, 74, 184
    social, 74
Agencies
    employment, 65, 157, 174
    job-search, 205-207
    temporary, 158
Applications, employment, 175
Assistance, job-search, 205-208
Awards and honors, 73-74, 119

Back-door approach, 156
Behavior, during the
    interview, 176
Better deal,
    negotiating for, 195-196
Blind ads, 156-157
Bolles, Richard Nelson, 30
Business, starting
    your own, 18, 66
Buzzwords, industry, 24

Career Card, 149

Career file, 57-60, 149
Case studies, 83-99
Changing careers,
    resume for, 96-99
Childcare experience, 121
Chronological format, 77-78,
    101-120, 136-137
Clarity, on resume, 68, 101
Classified ads, 22, 155-157
Clothes, for the
    interview, 174-175
Cold-contact marketing, 152-155
College graduates,
    resume for, 92-93
Company-paid seminars, 117-118
Computer, personal, 141-142
Consultants, employment, 157
Contacts
    job, 25-26
    mail, 155
    networking, 147-155, 173-174
Contracts, termination, 194
Copies, making, 143
Corporate ladder,
    moving up, 94-95
Cover letters, 159-167

Design strategies, 125-131
Diplomacy, 177-178
Discounts, employee, 193
Discrimination, sexual, 15-16

"Don'ts," resume, 74-76
*Do What You Love, The Money Will Follow*, 30
Drop-outs, from the work force, 16-17

Editing, your resume, 133-139
Education, 37, 112-116, 137
Effective resume, requirements for, 68
Elements, of a resume, 69-76, 101-124, 135
Employee discounts, 193
Employer input, 202-203
Employment
  agencies, 65, 157, 174
  applications, 175
  consultants, 157
Equality, in the workplace, 15-19
Etiquette, during the interview, 176
Executive search firms, 157, 174
Expenses, moving, 194
Experience
  childcare, 121
  management, 121-122
  professional, 34-35, 106-112
  profile, 136-137
  timeline, 122
  volunteer, 35-37, 73, 84-89, 106-112

Failure, 180
Family status, 186-187
File, career, 57-60, 149
Firing, explaining in an interview, 185
Firms, executive search, 157, 174
First-timers
  resume for, 16-17, 90-93
  interview tips for, 184-185
Follow-up
  after the interview, 187-188
  calls, 167-170

Formats, resume, 77-82, 101-124, 134, 136-137
Friends, 204
Functional format, 78-81, 120-124, 136-137

Gaps, in employment history, 16-17, 183-184
Glass Ceiling Commission, 15-16
Goals, career, 32-33, 101, 182
Grade point average (GPA), 115

Hauter, Janet, 17
Headhunters, 157-158
High school education, 114-115
Hobbies, 119-120
Honors and awards, 73-74, 119
Housewife, resume for, 90-91
Human Resources (HR), 23-25
Hybrid format, 81, 136-137

Information interviews, request for, 159-161
Input, employer, 202-203
Insurance benefits, 193
Interests, outside, 73, 119-120
Interviewing, 171-188
  questions, 176-187
Interviews, 150
  information, 159-161
Inventory, taking, 33-56

Job
  contacts, 25-26
  leads, 148ff
  objective, 71-72, 104-105, 120, 136
  references, 75
Job offer, responding to, 192-200
Job-search
  resources, 205-208
  strategies, 147-158

Layoff, explaining in an interview, 185

Leadership positions,
 resume for, 94-95
Leads, job, 148ff
Length, of resume, 102, 134
Library references, 207-208
Licensing, professional, 116-117
Loans, using your resume for, 66

Mail
 contacts, 155
 selling by, 159-170
Management experience, 121-122
Marketing tool, 63-68
Marketing, yourself, 26-28
Mass mailing, 22-23
*Megatrends 2000*, 18
*Megatrends for Women,* 18
Memberships and
 activities, 118-119
Military service, 37-38
Modesty, 177
Money, 31
Moving expenses, 194

Naisbitt, John, 18
Name header,
 on resume, 103-104, 120, 135
Negotiating, 189-200
Networking, 25-26, 65,
 147-152, 173-174, 204
Newsletter subscription, 208
Nice girl syndrome, 17

Objective opinion,
 getting an, 203
Objective, job, 71-72, 120, 136
Open-ended questions, 179
Opportunities, job, 18
Options, stock, 194
Outside interests, 73, 119-120
Overtime policies, 193

Paper stock, used for
 resume, 143-144
Personal statistics, 75

Personality
 assessing, 182-183
 profiles, 75
Personnel department, 23-25
Phone prospecting, 154
Photos, on resume, 75
Post-secondary education, 113-114
Printing, your resume, 141-144
Professional affiliations, 74
Professional experience, 106-112
Professional licensing, 116-117
Profile, skill and experience,
 120-122, 136-137
Profit-sharing plans, 193
Proofreading,
 your resume, 139
Prospecting, phone, 154
Punctuality, 175-176
Punctuation, on resume, 102-103

Qualifications, 68
 summary of, 72, 105
Questions, interview, 176-187

Recruiting firm, 174
References, 75, 174
Rejection, handling, 201-204
Researching
 a company, 171-174
 salaries, 189-190
Resources, 204-208
Resume
 action-oriented
  words on, 102, 111
 as a marketing tool, 63-68
 design strategies, 125-131
 "don'ts," 74-76
 editing, 133-139
 elements of, 69-76, 101-124, 135
 formats, 77-82
 length, 102, 134
 listing GPA on, 115
 making copies of, 143
 name header, 135
 printing, 141-144

proofreading, 139
punctuation on, 102-103
Q & A, 122-124
writing a rough draft of, 101-124
Retirement plans, 193
Rules, employment, 21-28

Salary
  negotiation, 189-200
  objections, 196
Salary information,
  on resume, 76
Sans serif typeface, 127-128
Satisfaction, career, 29-38
Self-assessment, 66
Self-inventory, 33-56
Serif typeface, 127-128
Service, military, 37-38
Services, employment, 157-158
Sexual harassment, in an
  interview, 185
Sinetar, Marsha, 30
Skill and experience
  profile, 120-122
Skills summary, 38, 105-106,
  120, 136
Skills, special, 37-38
Social affiliations, 74
Special education
  experiences, 115-116
Stationary, for resume, 144
Stock options, 194
Strategies, job-search, 147-158
Strategy, reviewing your, 203
Strengths and weaknesses, 179

Summary of qualifications, 72, 105
Summary, skills, 136

Targeting your market, 27
Temporary agencies, 158
Termination contract, 194
Testimonials, on resume, 76
Thanking
  contacts, 151
  interviewers, 187-188
Timeline, experience, 122
Tips, for better-looking
  resumes, 127-131
Training and certification, 116-117
Tuition reimbursement, 193
Typefaces, 127-128
Typesetting, your resume, 143
Typewriter, office-quality, 142

Updating your resume, 67, 74

Vacation days, 193
Volunteer experience, 35-37,
  73, 84-89, 106-112, 184-185

*What Color is Your
  Parachute?*, 30
Word processor,
  professional, 142-143
Word-of-mouth, 148-152
Words, action-oriented, 102, 111
Work experience, 34-35, 106-112
Worksheets,
  self-inventory, 34-56
Worth, knowing your, 189-190